THE MAKING OF
A GEM &
The Apple of His Eye

By Ambassador Tina Black

THE MAKING OF
A GEM &
The Apple of His Eye

Destiny of a Chocolate Doll Baby 5
Featuring a 12 Day Victory Plan

By Ambassador Tina Black

THE MAKING OF A GEM & The Apple of His Eye

(Destiny of a Chocolate Doll Baby 5 Featuring a 21 Day Victory Plan)

Other Publications by Ambassador Tina Black

Destiny of a Chocolate Doll Baby ½ & 3,4

Christians Love Life

Time 2 P.U.S.H.

Stay at Home Tea Journal (for ladies)

Stay at Home Coffee Journal (for men)

Stay at Home Snack & Juice Box Journal (for kids)

The Intercessors Domain
Invitation to the Clarion Call
Sequel *to TIME 2 P.U.S.H.!*

The Prayer Warriors and Intercessors Handbook

Cover Design: CreateSpace.com, an Amazon Company

Biblical references from the translation to English are quoted from the King James Version. Unless otherwise noted. Reference books listed on back.

Printed in the United States of America

Category: Christian living, Encouragement, Warfare, Prophetic,
           Declarative, Prayer, Intercession, Testimonial, Fasting

ISBN:9781530150939

Table of Contents

<u>*Authors Note & Word of Encouragement*</u>

My Dearsest Reader, I am so excited about this project.

Seems like it took all winter, most certainly the entire Holiday season to write this book. It has been a tough assignment but an interesting one as well, if that makes sense. I depended on the leadd of the Lord to help me to explain this season to the Chocolate Doll baby;s Journey, for I wanted to share the Word of God that has been shared with me by Him through the years.

It wasn't about a particular service that I was in or a message that I heard, but the timing of God as He dealt with me on a personal one-on-one. It was times when He Himself was loving on me and satisfying me with the good sincere meat of His Word.

&&&&&&&&

With a heartfelf act of humbleness and gratitude, I dedicate this book to all who feel the stretching, the re-fining, the pounding. For this is the season when God has poured out of His Spirit upon all flesh that will receive al-ready. This book I write for the ones who feel the shaking and moving in your spirit, and you can say without doubt, that God is preparing us for GREATER.

I BELIEVE THAT A TRUMP OF GOD HAS SOUNDED, and there is an exodus, influx, a flowing of the Spirit of God moving upon and in His people in this hour. We are in this hour being made as gemstones in the kingdom. In this moving that is taking place right now, God is letting us know just how precious we are to Him. He is making us to shine in a dark world more than ever before. In this season we will stand as Apples of His Eye, chosen, being perfected as we walk in obedience to His lead.

Lastly, we had to be refined in the manner in which we have come in order to step into a pre-ordained sequencial place of order for such a time as this. Selah!

1994

"You are precious to me, you are the apple of my eye!"

I guess I had grown up some, taken a leap of faith. Being led by my spiritual head, my husband, Elder Pete Black, then a licensed ordained Deacon in the Pentecostal Assemblies of the World, "PAW". Me, I was a trained Missionary, National Prayer Warrior, Minister in Training, and faithful Choir Member. We had just relocated to my hometown, my birthplace, where I'd been kidnapped from 31 years prior. We moved from Cali to Laurel, Mississippi in 1991.

We were fellow-shipped into Trueway Apostolic Church some 35 miles from Laurel in a larger city, Hattiesburg, Mississippi, under the Pastorate of Elder Abraham Yarbrough, Sr.. Trueway as we called it was an anointed seedbed for a spiritually hungry and thirsty saint, who desired to grow and do great things for the Kingdom. One of my assignments, I was blessed to work as Pastor Yarbrough's personal secretary. I've only written checks for thousands of dollars once or twice in my life and they were during the season that I spent with Pastor Yarbrough.

The five years that we spent at Trueway, my husband, and our four children, were the years that God allowed me to be nutured. I was far from home, away from the familiar walls of Greater Bethany Community Church of L.A.,

CA where we were three to five-thousand strong on Sunday mornings. The two assemblies were on opposite ends of the scale in a lot of ways, but, one thing they had in common was that they both had Spirit filled, driven leaders who loved God and His people.

The lay members were similar as well, for they loved God, they were humble, and there was a group of people within the assembly that not only embraced God, but they loved to PRAY. They would pray all night, they would pray at noon, they would pray at State Meetings as well as National Meetings. We were placed over the Missionary Auxiliary, we knew the WORD, and next in line was Prayer, we loved to pray.

God had placed us with an awesome group of ladies, just as He had promised. When the call was answered to come to Mississippi, the prophecy as we now know had come forth, that there would be people here to meet us. They were, and they were faithful ones being members of the body, from the Pastorate to the door. They were a blessing to us in so many ways, mentally, spiritually, and financially, they were indeed the people that God had designated to meet us.

We were in a great place spiritually, the Word was going forth, I was getting plenty of personal, one on one nuturing from Elder Yarbrough. I had the experience of a season of an open heaven, God was downloading information faster than I could receive, and much of which I did not understand. As I would share what God gave me with Elder Y., he would explain it to me and then, give me a scripture, toooooo, back it up. My, God!!!!!

I didn't know ANYTHING about Prophecy back then, to know what was Prophetic. I knew that, I was having dreams and visions and I could hear an audible voice of God speaking to me, especially when I would pray. I would pray hard, as I called it, till God would take me into a heavy tongue, I had the gift of prophecy, according to what I know today. I did not know how to equate what I was hearing audibly to what I was speaking. I did not fully understand the gift of Interpretation.

One day during Noon-day prayer, I began to feel as if I was being torn or separated. I learned that God was trying to get me to separate my natural hearing from my spiritual ear. I got stuck, and began to cry out, "Lord, what is it?" He said to me over and over, "You are the apple of my eye." As I would hear, I began to see. There was a case in front of me, in a vision, in the Spirit, my eyes were closed, locked shut. I begin to see something red, hanging from a gold string. As I focused in, I saw that it was the prettiest, red, marble looking apple. The case was made of beveled glass, and I could see the apple, it was turning as if it was rotating. That was the prettiest, awesome-mist, beautiful-iest apple I have ever seen. (I took the liberty of trying to put some awesome apples on the cover, they don't compare to the one I saw).

I could hear a voice saying over and over, "You are the apple of my eye!" I had to write it down. Afterwards, usually when God deals with me on that order, I have to write it down quickly, lest I forget. As soon as we dismissed, I made my way to Elder Y. and shared my vision and the voice that I heard. Elder Y. took me to the scriptures below, I am going to share with you, my dear reader, the info of flow that was given to me. This really encouraged me I pray that it is a blessing to you..

ZEC2.6-11 Ho, ho, come forth, and flee from the land of the north, saith the LORD: for I have spread you abroad as the four winds of the heaven, saith the LORD.
7 Deliver thyself, O Zion, that dwellest with the daughter of Babylon.

3

*8 For thus saith the LORD of hosts; After the glory hath he sent me unto the nations which spoiled you: **for he that toucheth you toucheth the apple of his eye.***
9 For, behold, I will shake mine hand upon them, and they shall be a spoil to their servants: and ye shall know that the LORD of hosts hath sent me.
10 Sing and rejoice, O daughter of Zion: for, lo, I come, and I will dwell in the midst of thee, saith the LORD.
11 And many nations shall be joined to the LORD in that day, and shall be my people: and I will dwell in the midst of thee, and thou shalt know that the LORD of hosts hath sent me unto thee. KJV

There are other passages that confirm the blessing of our being the apple of God's eye. The Wikepedia dictionary says; The phrase *apple of my eye* refers to something or someone that one cherishes above all others. To know that God loves us so much that He would use such a term of endearment was sooo special. I felt divinely protected.

There is nothing like confirmation in Gods WORD. There are many other scriptures that speak of one being the Apple of God's eye. King David had a turn many times in his life to be referred to as the Apple of God's eye. I have enjoyed and loved my life, being the apple of the Lords eye. His favor has been un-comparable towards us through the years. Oh, how I bless Him.

2004

"They are Gems in the Kingdom"

I didn't understand why my husband and I were being referred to as a Gems in the Kingdom. We were said to be dedicated and faithful, to that which we were a part of. In this case it was church. We both had been raised in church, trained to be good honest hearted people, which seemed natural. Especially since we were in service for the Lord. Even to this day we still ask the question, "What made us love God like we did, what were we taught that was so different of today?"

Whatever it was, we praise God that it is still with us to-day. Neither one of us would take nothing for our journey. I'm sure that I speak for my husband. The tests and the tri-als do not outweigh the blessings and glory that we have experienced. Besides trials come and go, and in the process, we have become wiser, stronger and more deter-mined to run on and see what the end will be.

*Let us be mindful that there is a difference between gemstone and jewel...*the gemstone is refrred to as a gem, it is usually made of minerals while a jewel is a precious or semi-precious stone; gem, gemstone. Both are precious to Him, for He made them for His Glory.

Thus, I begun my private tutoring and study sessions with the greatest teacher, the Holy Ghost. The one thing I love most about God is that He will expose me to something, then urge me and lead me into a revealing and uncovering victorious study.

I learned to use a Concordance early in my kingdom walk. One of the first scriptures of study was *Ezekiel 28.13 Thou hast been in Eden the garden of God; every precious stone was thy covering, the sardius, topaz, and the diamond, the beryl, the onyx, and the jasper, the sapphire, the emerald, and the carbuncle, and gold: the workmanship of thy tabrets and of thy pipes was prepared in thee in the day that thou wast created. KJV*

The scripture spoke of some of the most precious jewels that God ever created. I looked at their meanings, their effects, and their uses. The Emerald stood out most for me, it is my birthstone. God took me back to some of His most precious servants of the scriptures. Naomi, Esther, Anna, Sara, all three Mary's, Eve, and the list continues. And for my husband, there was Adam, David, Moses, Joshua, Peter, and that list could go on and on, as well.

In the natural, *Gemstones* are minerals/rocks found beneath the earths surface that are polished and made into jewelry or collected. They can be very valuable and rare. Diamonds are considered a gemstone.

Gems are mined from the earth in various methods around the planet. These gems are separated from the unwanted material at the mine. The unrefined gems will be then sorted for size and quality, larger stones will be separated out to be treated specially in efforts to maximise value. Stones that are deemed to be of a high enough quality will go on to the gem smith where they will be cut to size according to the type of cut needed. Some of these cutting steps are, planning, and cleaving or sawing, bruting, and polishing.

Why did we share this, those that are prophetic will see a correlation here with that of the refining and preparation process of a saint of God. Going deeper, upon His lead, His instructions, I found this piece that inspired and gave seasonal insight to my search, I share...

Arthur W. Pink (1886-1952) - "And they shall be Mine, says the Lord Almighty, in that day when I make up My jewels" (Mal. 3:17). To whom is God here referring? Who are the favored ones whom He terms His "jewels"? The previous verse tells us, "Then those who feared the Lord talked with each other, and the Lord listened and heard. A scroll of remembrance was written in his presence concerning those who feared the Lord and honored his name." A twofold description is there given by which the people of God may be identified: they have a reverential awe and profound respect of God's majesty and authority;

7

they have a deep love and adoration for Him—
evidenced by their thinking upon His name.

It almost surprises one to learn that the great and
self-sufficient God has "jewels," but our surprise
increases to astonishment when we learn that
these "jewels" are living creatures, and
astonishment gives place to overwhelming
amazement when we discover that these living
creatures are fallen and depraved sinners
redeemed from among the children of men. Truly,
nothing but Divine grace would ever liken such
wretched worms of the dust, unto precious
stones. Yet that is the very thing which we find
God doing in our text. It is not the unfallen
angels, nor the holy seraphim and exalted
cherubim who are spoken of as Jehovah's valued
treasure, but lost and ruined sinners saved by
amazing grace!

Saints are likened unto wheat, fish,trees, stars,
but here to "jewels"; the figure is a deeply
interesting and instructive one. In Isaiah 55:8-9
we read, "For My thoughts are not your thoughts,
neither are your ways My ways, says the Lord. For
as the heavens are higher than the earth, so are
My ways higher than your ways, and My thoughts
than your thoughts."

The world's standard of worth is very different
from that of God's. Who are the immortals of
human history? Caesar, Charlemagne, Napoleon:
soldiers and warriors. Among statesmen and
politicians we may mention Gladstone and
Lincoln: among dramatists, Goethe and
Shakespeare. Those were great in the eyes of
earth; but who were great in the eyes of Heaven?

8

For the most part they were unknown down here.They were humble and lowly, insignificant in the affairs of the world. Their names were never chronicled among men; but they were written in the Lamb's Book of Life!

So it is now when all godly testimony has broken down, when Christendom is in spiritual ruins. Many of God's dear children no longer have the privilege of church fellowship, for they dare not attend the modern "synagogues of Satan." But some of them still have the joy of meeting with little groups of fellow pilgrims, seeking to strengthen one another's hands as they journey through this wilderness scene. But there are others of God's "scattered" (John 11:52) saints, who are cut off from practically all real Christian fellowship, isolated ones, who have to mourn with David, "I watch, and am as a sparrow alone upon the housetop" (Psalm 102:7). Yet, though they can no longer "speak often one to another," they still have the holy and blessed privilege of thinking upon that Name which is above every name.

These, too, shall be numbered among His precious treasure in the day when He shall "make up His jewels." Did we possess these qualities. Was our mindset aligned to this description, we had to testify, yes, yes, yes. Out of all that we went through till now, we had to give a nod, of we were glad to be referred to as gems of the Kingdom.

One once wrote: "Earthly jewels sometimes get separated from their owner, Christ's jewels never: 'For I am persuaded, that neither death, nor life . ..

nor any other creature, shall be able to separate us from the love of God, which is in Christ Jesus our Lord' (Romans 8:38, 39). Earthly jewels are sometimes lost—Christ's jewels never: 'I give unto them eternal life; and they shall never perish, neither shall any man pluck them out of My hand' (John 10:28). Earthly jewels are sometimes stolen —Christ's jewels never: 'in Heaven, where neither moth nor rust does corrupt, and where thieves do not break through nor steal' (Matt. 6:20)."

Are you sure that you are one of Christ's gems or jewels? Then seek to shine for Him now.

Chapter 1

Deep Calleth Unto Deep
Psalms 42:7

The year was 1987, I knelt at the altar. The sanctuary of then Greater Bethany Community Church, Los Angeles, California was quiet that day. I'm not gonna say as a church house mouse, for I really don't know if we had one. I was the only soul stirring, it was my assignment as a choir member and junior prayer warrior to dust the altar and the pulpit furniture.

I moistened the dusting towel with the oil, and began praying as God instructed, and wiped the banister. I was careful, making sure that I didn't miss any of it. I worked at a pace across the banister portion, then the poles. What an awesome spirit of peace that rested around me.

I moved toward the pulpit working efficiently as my task was well uder way. You see I had a plan, I was going to go up, do the pulpit, then, come down and start on the portion of the altar on the left side of the podium. God instructed me to continue on the altar, to cross over to the other side and not go up to the pulpit, just yet. I had my view on the podium, the piano, and the Bishops chair. I had my idea of order, I thought that I was organized and knew the best way to get this job done, but, God let me know that day that He had a plan and His plan was the plan to follow.

I was in a real big hurry, and I really wanted to move along.

My way was not going to work in this task, God had another plan. I obeyed the voice of the Lord, I backed down the steps and began wiping the altar again, not knowing what the delay would entail. As I continued I began hearing in my spirit what sounded like wailing and weeping. The sound became clearer and distinct. I began to pray for what I was hearing. Praying that the Lord would bless and heal those whose weeping and wailing I'd heard.

I asked the Lord to intervene to answer their cries. As I did so, some of the sounds became joyful cries and weeping mixed with daughter. I finished the altar dusting task that day with joy and peace. Some folk would've taken flight, but, I wasn't afraid, I had a sense to remain still. Some people may have thought that they were going crazy, hearing voices, but there was a peace about this happening. I left the church that day with a made up mind to ask the committee leaders for the same assignment the next week, I felt like God was going to really show me something in this. Glory!

I went home, while doing my chores and winding up my day with my children, I heard the Lord speak these words; *"Deep calleth unto deep!"*
What would these words mean to me, I was learning that God deals with us as we submit ourselves to Him, so, He was going to teach me a lesson here. As we listen, He speaks. As He speak, it would do us well to listen and hear in order to ultimately obey. There is an essence in obedience. For, it is always better than sacrifice. There is a plan that our Lord has,

His plans are to always supersede our plans. We must be ready and willing to receive what God has in store for us. In searching, I quickly arrived at the scripture that held these precious words. Lo, and behold it was a scripture! But, what would it mean, what would it say to me in the coming days.

> *PSA42.7 Deep calleth unto deep at the noise of thy waterspouts: all thy waves and thy billows are gone over me.*

The scripture was; Deep calleth unto deep. It became embedded in my spirit. I could not, nor did I want to shake it. Time passed and I meditated on this powerful scripture. It had taken root and was ready to settle.

As time grew, and I spent more time on the altar, my spirit began to open more and more. In submission to the Spirit of God, there was a lightning, weight-lifting effect that took place within my spirit. God began to show Himself mighty. One Sunday morning, Bishop Mac took his stand and we know...what the scripture was. He explained of how the deepness of God would call unto the deepness in us. He said that God's Spirit would call out to the spirit in man, and once they have made connection man could not help but cry out "yes" to the True and Living God.

After that message, I had a Yes in my spirit that I knew only God could put there of His own good pleasure. Our heavenly Father wants us, He desires us, so He Himself implants a Yes and a Want-to in us that connects with the breath of life that He gave to us. As it is activated, we will give forth a yes, even when we don't know we're saying yes.

We'll be singing, "Soul says yes, yes Lord...Soul cry out, yes Lord, Yes to your will Lord, Yes Lord, Yes, to Your way, Lord, I'll obey, each and every day!!!"

There develops within a deep thunderous desire to please Him, in all of our ways.

The Bible says in Philippians 2:13, *For it is God which worketh in you both to will and to do of his good pleasure.* In other words God's Spirit goes deep inside us to our inward parts and worketh in us both to will and to do of His good pleasure.

When we are overtaken as the latter portion of the scripture of Psalms 42:7 says, we are overtaken and compelled to do what is pleasing to God.

Oh! How how I've learned to be compelled to walk pleasing Him, I've learned to talk pleasing Him. I've learned to give myself away, totally committed to Him. That same deepness still calls unto me today, it's been 35 years since I recognized that voice. That voice had been calling unto me from my days as a child in the country of Altair, but it wasn't until maturity came that I realized who was calling. Now, at age 58 I can say, Lord, here am I, send me, for-real.

Chapter 2
Is This A Call for
Communion and Intimacy?

Through dedicated prayer and study God began to reveal
the essence of this passage. He let me know or revealed
that within the "Deep" there was He and I.

There would come a form of communion that I could only
experience with Him. This would be an act of intimacy
and exchange that would take me through, get this, to the
next "deep." "Deeper!!!"

One priceless lesson I learned was that, with God there is
no play with words. Only rich integrity of the gospel that
can only be found with His precious Holy Word. I
realized that God was actually wanting me to get to know
Him better. I was His creation, He knew all about me –
He merely wanted an acknowledgment from me that He
could ultimately trust me with the deep things of His.

Even as I am penning now, I hear the Lord saying, that
He has concerns of reaching a depth of communion with
us that will be so at one that we will operate in the Spirit
of unity of faith and Spirit. We will b e intertwined with
Him.

Allow the Spirit to lead...We do not need to take this call
to commune with our Heavenly Father lightly. As we
yield ourselves to the Holy Spirit, He will lead us. The
Word of the Lord says to us in 1 Corinthians 2:9-13 ;

1CO2.9 But as it is written, Eye hath not seen, nor ear heard, neither have entered into the heart of man, the things which God hath prepared for them that love him. 1CO2.10 But God hath revealed them unto us by his Spirit: **for the Spirit searcheth all things, yea, the deep things of God.** *1CO2.11 For what man knoweth the things of a man, save the spirit of man which is in him? even so the things of God knoweth no man, but the Spirit of God. 1CO2.12 Now we have received, not the spirit of the world, but the spirit which is of God; that we might know the things that are freely given to us of God. 1CO2.13 Which things also we speak, not in the words which man's wisdom teacheth, but which the Holy Ghost teacheth; comparing spiritual things with spiritual.*

There are places in God that we will only reach by answering the call to commune with Him. This season of communion does not just include the breaking of the bread and partaking of the wine, although this is not a place to be ignored. This goes deeper and deals with revelation, knowledge. *Verse 10 says, but God hath revealed them unto us by his Spirit: for the Spirit searcheth all things, yea, the deep things of God.*

Without the Spirit of God, we will miss this experience and will not receive from the deep things of God. It is a must that embrace more than surface knowledge. We must indulge in His Spirit and seek Him for greater.

I realize more so now and I am grateful for having answered his call. This was a call to come-into-union with the Lord. It was time for me to come into a place of union with the divine. At the time I felt like a wretch undone who was being called higher and deeper at the same time.

There was a deep place in God that only a few desire to go. My question was, "Can I walk in this place of Communion?" I had this thought, what was there so deep in me that My God referred to as deep and desirous that I would come into unity with Him.

What was He looking for and did I really have it. God revealed to me to that the moment that I was feeling had already been set in time. He had set this moment in place before I was in my mothers womb. So, I had been chosen to be one of the ones whose desires would be to commune with Him. I was born this way. And, I do speak in tongues, right here, Lord, God, I bless You!!!

To me my life was a wreck. I had barely walked out of the Nickerson Gardens by way of Jordan Downs both Housing Projects, in the midst outside of Watts, or South Central L.A. My God, I had not been the model saint. Yet, God wanted me. He had touched that place deep inside of me where there was a mechanism in operation that had been ignited and was drawing me to Him as He was calling me to Him. Oh, My God!

Yes, this was a call for communion. My Heavenly Father was calling me – He had great plans for me – At the time I was not in position to even imagine my latter. He has awesome plans for you, my dear reader as well.

Chapter 3
The Spirit of the Bride says COME!
Revelations 22:17

The New Living Translation says...*The Spirit and the Bride say, "Come," Let anyone who hears this say, "Come." Let anyone who is thirsty come. Let anyone who desires drink freely from the water of life. NLT*

Once I realized that this christian walk is a never-ending walk, things began to line up or should I say became aligned. Allow me to explain. My own personal lifes plans were to become a Fashion Designer. When I was nine and ten years old, I drew pages and pages of shoes that look like the shoes that are being worn today. Stacked, plat-formed with straps, the works. I would draw clothing designs and turn around and make them for my Barbie dolls.

At this point of my journey when I received this scripture, I would say that I was well on my way to becoming that designer that I desired to be. I was taking Merchandising and Design classes at Los Angeles Trade Tech College. I felt as if God had given me gifting for one thing, but now with new desires deriving from deep within was changing those plans.

I'd always desired to sew, it was part of that Fashion Design Gift. He had blessed me with a Sewing Machine, Fabric and a Pattern from J.C. Penny, I was what *I thought*, well on *my* way. We live in a season to accept the fact that God has a right to change His mind, and to change our plans. Many are the plans of a mans heart, but it is the will of the Lord that shall prevail, *my translation!*

Get all the advice and instruction you can, so you will be wise the rest of your life. You can make many plans, but the LORD's purpose will prevail. Proverbs 19:20-21 NLT

Our plans versus the will of the Lord can be delayed, put-off or just flat out canceled. We seek Him, His advice, His instructions. We do this early in life, how early depends on how long one wants to be wise and prosperous. It is up to the individual, our God allows us free will to make our choices, in some cases. In others we are miserable and unhappy until we give God a yes!

So, we can begin as a child, as soon as we come into understanding of Him and His directives or His Word. This in itself would be wise, for if we wait later in life, we may become wise in our own eyes or weak and wise with worldly views. Thus, it would be difficult to differentiate God's directives from the knowledge that we have acquired at the hand of education or having been around those who were not Godly.

Later in life, mid twenties to mid thirties, is a difficult age to adjust to the things of God if we are not Spirit filled. Why do we say this, because our minds have been so formed and shaped with the experiences that we have been exposed to. In this case the soulish man has been silenced for years and our physical man has been in charge for a long time. The best way to measure and compare the two is to see how one responds to spiritual things. Which one is the strongest, which one has more dominance in ones life.

There is a measuring stick that I love to use, I refer to it often in my own Christian walk. This ruling will shoot straight to the point. It is found in Galatians 5, we will pen it here. Take a look at which spirits or attributes or more dominate, and one will see just how spiritual they really are.

...And the Spirit gives us desires that are the opposite of what the sinful nature desires. These two forces are constantly fighting each other, so you are not free to carry out your good intentions. 18But when you are directed by the Spirit, you are not under obligation to the law of Moses. 19When you follow the desires of your sinful nature, the results are very clear: sexual immorality, impurity, lustful pleasures, 20idolatry, sorcery, hostility, quarreling, jealousy, outbursts of anger, selfish ambition, dissension, division, 21envy, drunkenness, wild parties, and other sins like these. Let me tell you again, as I have before, that anyone living that sort of life will not inherit the Kingdom of God. 22But the Holy Spirit produces this kind of fruit in our lives: love, joy, peace, patience, kindness, goodness, faithfulness, 23gentleness, and self-control. There is no law against these things! 24Those who belong to Christ Jesus have nailed the passions and desires of their sinful nature to his cross and crucified them there. 25Since we are living by the Spirit, let us follow the Spirit's leading in every part of our lives. 26Let us not become conceited, or provoke one another, or be jealous of one another. Galatians 5:...17-26 NLT

It would behoove us to perform a general temple cleaning, we will call it, at least once or twice a month or as often as we feel need. This is to make sure none of these works of the flesh have crept in. It is to make sure that the fruit of the spirit is still reigning in our lives It's not hard to slide to the negative side. One thing that will keep us and hold us fast is genuine fervent prayer, true praise, and truthful worship.

At any interval of our lives, we can hear the Spirit of the Lord, pulling us, calling us. There will be a continual ringing in our ears that simply says, "Come." It's when we approach another level, dimension, plateau, or plane of His Glory, that still small voice comes. In His speaking, there is an action that occurs, we refer to it as, "catapault." In other words, God seems to pick us up and set us over into another place or space of His time. We have the experience of the Ethiopian eunuch. We are here, then the next area of alertness, we are there, and don't know how we arrived. But, we can stand flat-footed with asurity and declare that nobody but God could have brought this act to pass.

I've declared more than once during this journey that there is an attitude on "the call" that is released during ones walk to the altar that does not end until we have reached eternity. For as long as we live, breath and serve, there is a continual release of "Yes, Lord, I come, I come to thee!" hold that is on us. Why else would He remind us that, In Him, we move, live and have our (total) being.

When our dear friends, family or co-workers contact us via the phone, e-mail, twitter, snap-chat or face-book us, at some point we hang up and disconnect or un-friend for a period of time. When our Lord and Savior calls, we never have the opportunity to put Him on hold, let alone hang up or disconnect. Jesus is the only entity that I know of that can call us, and we can look at the caller-ID and say, I ain't gonna answer that. When the Spirit and the Bride says come, we might as well not hardened our hearts. We might as well join in and sing one of my favorite songs, "Something down inside of me, telling me to go ahead, go ahead, go ahead, go ahead..." If we do otherwise, that explains some of our dispositions and deli-mas. Selah!

I do believe that I will shout right there, all by myself!!!!!

Chapter 4
The Element

#449. Elements—The basic, essential parts of something. Prophetically pertains to the composite subjects, substances, or disciplines that generate the activities vital to its purpose.

#4747. stoy-khi'-on neuter of a presumed derivative of the base of stoy-kheh'-o ; something orderly in arrangement, i.e. (by implication) a serial (basal, fundamental, initial) constituent (literally), proposition (figuratively): element, principle, rudiment. Strong, James (2010-09-15). Strong's Dictionary of the Bible. Greek and Hebrew Kindle Edition.

English – A part or aspect of something abstract, especially one that is essential or characteristic.

And, Ohhhh, how I love this definition...A fundamental, essential, or irreducible, constituent of a composites entity. Farlex Dictionary

God dropped this word into my spirit – He said that within each one of us lies an element. The analogy that actually brought me to this point was – when my feet had barely rested on Mississippi soil, I had a dryer and a stove to go out simultaneously. When the neighborhood handyman who worked on appliances came to fix them, he said to me, "Ms Black, yo element done gone out on both the dryer and the stove."
Okay, quite naturally, I asked what was an element.

He said, "That there is the vital part that makes it go, neither one ain't getting no fye, they ain't being ignited, you see, without the element, they ain't gone work." He began clearing away items on the counter in his way, taking out a little notebook and a pen, he began to draw on the paper, then he stopped, looked me square in the face and said, "We each have a element in us, you can call it sponk, get up and go, or whatever you wanta call it, but if hit ain't litin, we ain't gone have no get-up about us."

See, he was not a preacher, in a church, he was wise, he read his Bible, so when he told me about that element, I could have tore my kitchen up, how profound.

I perceive this element to be the breath of God, see, it had to be something that gives life, I also looked at it as being zeal, and finally it had to be the Holy Ghost, God's Spirit. Now, we all know that with the integral part that causes the dryer to heat, it will turn and turn, but it won't get hot to dry the clothes. If the heating element goes out in the oven, we won't be able to bake biscuits, cakes, chicken, or cornbread.

Therefore, an element is very important and necessary to aid with the heating process of an appliance to make it work properly. Well, deep inside of each of us there is an element placed there by a living God. It can't be seen, but it can be detected. Bottom line, without "it" we won't have any fye (fire) to us. There comes the argumentative suggestive, "Is this element our heart, our breath, our brain?" I want to inform you that is is a part of all of those, but essentially it is the breath of God that touches that heart and cause it to beat. This breath is the element, that is referred to as "ruach" meaning His Breath or the breath of God.

When this breath comes in, the oxygen in it touches our hearts, you see on another note, His very Spirit comes in, there is a "dunamis" sparking effect that takes place within us.

The firing of this element causes action to come forth. Once connected there is a calling that causes us to want to connect with the Living God. This sparking effect causes us not to rest until we have communed with Him. It causes us to seek Him until we are in total communion with Him.

Allow me to break down Communion – (Come) into (Union). This is a coming together, we come into union with the True and Living God.

Oh, I Praise God, for this element that has been ignited within us, it make us want to get up, when we need to sit down. It causes us to run, when nobodys chasing us. It makes us shout, holler, dance, throw up our hands, fall to our knees, fall on our faces. It makes us want to talk right, live right, pray right, fast right, treat ourselves and our neighbor right!!! Oh, My God, I bless You, right here.

Let me say this, there is an inner fire. This element is that inner fire when ignited, we have power to witness, in our home, on our job, and in our community. We have what it takes to tell a dying world, that Jesus saves. When we have this genuine fire, we will crave communion with our Lord ans Savior. It will cause us to believe and never, ever doubt again. It brings a difference to our lives, we won't make covenant with everything and everybody. We will set a difference between right and wrong. We will make a difference between clean and unclean.

If it sounds as if I am repeating myself, believe me, I'm not. I'm writing what the Holy Ghost tells me to write, and I'm writing it exactly how He says it, He want's us to get this, for this is where we are hurting in the Kingdom most.

We are Kingdom citizens, God is establishing His government in the earth. We have prayed for centuries, Our Father, who art in heaven, hollowed be thy Name, in earth, as it is in heaven. Thy kingdom come, thy will be done, in earth as it is in heaven..."

Well, the season is here, the time is now, we must more than ever purpose in our hearts to walk the straight and narrow, for narrow is the way, we can't walk broad any more. Basics, will always be basics, God is the same yesterday, today, and forever. We who are embracing Kingdom-dom, must hold on to the basics of our fore-fathers. Embrace, the mantles of power that are falling earthward and continue.

After leading us and guiding us into all truths, this element not only encourage us to walk right, talk right, pray right, and think right. Oh, bless the Name of Jesus.

It brings life to a dead situation. It gives us life, and that more abundantly. I praise God, it draws us, it pushes us it leads us, Oh, my God!

Chapter 5
Master, Teach!!!

Mark 1:21-22
21Jesus and his companions went to the town of Capernaum.
When the Sabbath day came, he went into the synagogue and
began to teach.
22The people were amazed at his teaching, for he taught with real
authority—quite unlike the teachers of religious law.

Psalms 32:8The LORD says, "I will guide you along the best
pathway for your life. I will advise you and watch over you.
(Both passages from NLT)

PSA32.8 I will instruct thee and teach thee in the way which thou
shalt go: I will guide thee with mine eye. The Holy Bible, King James
Version (KJV)

According to Google, there are around 31,175 verses in
the Psalms. At the time God evidently needed just one
(Psalms 32:8) to move me into a place of certainty. I don't
remember exactly what I was going through, I can only
say it must have been a rough spot because of the validity
of the passage. It was my shot in the arm.

The Greek verb, "diasko" means to give instruction.
(Matthew 4:23; 9:35, Romans 12:7; 1 Corinthians 4:17;
1Timothy 2:12; 4:11) Jesus is our teacher, without anyone
or anything else being equal because of his trust in the
Word of God, and His being One with God. To teach
means to give information that will enable one to learn. To
instruct is similar, but it come with demonstration, a
showing of "how to," if you will. There is a way for us to
go.

Further instruction is given to us in the book of Proverbs, there is a passage that says, *"Trust in the Lord, with all thine heart and lean not to our own understanding. In all of our ways acknowledge Him, and He will direct our path." (Proverbs 3:5-6)* On another note, I've oft times referred to this passage as the Manual of our GPS, that is God Our Personal Savior.

One Sunday morning, I confess, I was browsing the Scriptures. Most of us do that while listening to the message, besides, I wasn't a real preacher then. I came across the scripture, Psalms 32:8, it became a gem of a scripture to me. I grabbed it, hung it around my neck, and have held onto it throughout the years.

There is a blessing in being teach-able and learn-able, I consider it a gift that should be listed in the run down of Galatians 5. Something new can be learned every day if we will allow ourselves to be taught, by the Holy Spirit. He is an excellent teacher because He always teach exactly what we need, not only what we want to hear. This occurs as we acknowledge Him.

Our Lord and Savior, Jesus is an "incomparable" teacher. One can go to school and acquire one dozen Masters on different subjects and never gain enough knowledge to out smart Him.

The last clause of Psalms 32:8 I receive as our God throwing in an extra, a freebie, that He won't even charge us for. It says that God is even promising to see for us with His eyes. I've learned to trust Him, and I encourage you to do the same. To believe in Him is of the essence – He will not lead us the wrong way, and He definitely will not lead us astray, He loves us that much.

So, we say, why are so many of us going a muck. Wandering in the wilderness without aim or direction.

What we hear from some of our pulpits now is weak jargon. Most of it does not give us the oomph to seek higher ground. There is so much Word available to us now, yet, it comes to us without power and conviction. We must be very careful in this season, to hold on to that which is Truth.

There is more entertainment in the service than we would see at a circus, therefore it doesn't have enough fire, anointing to hold anybody. On a common ground, Saints don't seek God like we should. Every other person in the pew, choir stand, and elsewhere, have their own agenda of what they feel should go on in the service. Morning service is a show, in most cases, evening service is non-existent. Prayer is done everywhere else but in church.

The local assembly is sometimes scanty in attendance on Sunday morning, because people are going to church on the phone, or what is referred to as Cyber Church. None of which I have a direct issue with, only the Bible says for us to forsake not the assembling of ourselves together. The primary reason for the coming together is for us to encourage one another.

We must get back to the Master teaching us. He teaches through His Word, His Spirit. A prophetic season of "New" is on the horizon. Only Christ can do a new thing with us and through us. We must acknowledge God as Father, Jesus as the Son, and the Holy Ghost and all three as One. Jesus said something that was so profound, He told the disciples that He and His Father are One, and He does nothing of His own account, only what the Father tells Him to do.

We must have the same stand. That is, we do nothing of ourselves, only what the Father tells us to do. Only what He has taught us has the power to stand. He said in His Word for us to testify of those things that we have both seen and heard. Those things that have been revealed to us through His Spirit.

Chapter 6
Going Deeper 1

1TH5.22 Abstain from all appearance of evil. 1TH5.23 And the very God of peace sanctify you wholly; and I pray God your whole spirit and soul and body be preserved blameless unto the coming of our Lord Jesus Christ. 1TH5.24 Faithful is he that calleth you, who also will do it. (KJV)

"Shun the very appearance of evil." In other words, "Stay away from (all) evil." Evil is ever present, I believe the Apostle Paul said it best...*ROM7.17-23, Now then it is no more I that do it, but sin that dwelleth in me. For I know that in me (that is, in my flesh,) dwelleth no good thing: for to will is present with me; but how to perform that which is good I find not. For the good that I would I do not: but the evil which I would not, that I do. Now if I do that I would not, it is no more I that do it, but sin that dwelleth in me. I find then a law, that, when I would do good, evil is present with me. For I delight in the law of God after the inward man: But I see another law in my members, warring against the law of my mind, and bringing me into captivity to the law of sin which is in my members. (KJV)*

Avoid evil. Even when we try with all of our might to do good, the Bible says that evil is always present. We began to realize that there is no good thing within us. It takes a made up mind being led of the Spirit to keep us from that evil. There is always a tug of war within us. I believe the Lord God purposes it to some degree, He wants us to be of our free will, and make the wise choice to follow hard after Him. He even promises upon repentance, our sins will be remitted, and we are promised the gift of the Holy

31

Ghost. (Acts 2:38) He will sanctify us wholly spirit, soul and body, and find us blameless until He come for us. (1 Thessalonians 5:23) The Holy Ghost will lead us and guide us into all truths, (St. John 16:13).

It is a known fact, that we don't have to look hard to find evil. Evil lurks in the shadows. It hovers, it is a spirit in the earth looking for someone to attach itself too. This is why the Lord tells us to shun the appearance of it. Everything is not always what it look like, or appears to be. We don't have to be afraid or nervous about this though, we need to rest more in the security of the Holy Ghost. Our God is an all seeing God, nothing is hid from Him. (Luke 8:17, Hebrews 4:13) Therefore, He knows all things.

Going deeper allowed me the greatest opportunity to include some powerful Word in my spiritual diet. These are just a few scriptures that enabled me to shun the appearance of evil. As I reflect on them, I do pray that they are a blessing to you as well.

Psalms 119:10,11 - With my whole heart have I sought thee: O let me not wander from thy commandments. Thy word have I hid in mine heart, that I might not sin against thee. KJV

With my whole heart, I decided to seek the Lord, I was drawn to His awesomeness. I love the portion of this scripture that says, O Let me not wander from thy commandments, in other words, Lord, help me not to wander, from the words that you have given me. In addition, I've tucked the word away in my heart, it will help me to stay focused, the word will help me not to go astray. Having the word hidden in my heart will detour me from sinning. (Psalms 119:11)

Romans 12:1,2 - I beseech you therefore, brethren, by the mercies of God, that ye present your bodies a living sacrifice, holy, acceptable unto God, which is your reasonable service. And be not conformed to this world: but be ye transformed by the renewing of your mind, that ye may prove what is that good, and acceptable, and perfect, will of God. KJV

I love the word beseech, it means; I summon, entreat, admonish, comfort
Definition: (a) I send for, summon, invite, (b) I beseech, entreat, beg, (c) I exhort, admonish, (d) I comfort, encourage, console.
3870 *parakaléō* (from **3844** /*pará*, "*from* close-beside" and **2564** /*kaléō*, "to call") – properly, "make a call" from being "close-up and personal." **3870** /*parakaléō* ("personally make a call") refers to believers *offering up evidence* that *stands up in God's court*. [**3870** (*parakaléō*), the root of **3875** /*paráklētos* ("*legal* advocate"), likewise has *legal* overtones.] (Strongs Concordance)

It's as though, I could hear the Lord say, "I summon you to present your body..." (I could hear the Lord say, with a calm hand) I need you to keep your body in tact for me." Keep it pure, holy, so it can be offered in service to me, this is the least you can do. Don't be like the world, don't think like them, walk like them, talk like them. Be changed everyday by renewing your mind in order to prove to me what is good and acceptable to me.

I had to go deeper, separate my self, become set apart. I realized that I was given this body that I occupy for His use. He did not care about my personal accomplishments as I did. He was concerned about my soul and the impact that I would make on someone elses walk in Him.

Allow us to deal with the area of separating ourselves and being set apart. There is a discipline that come about when one dedicate themselves and declare that they are only for the Masters use. Within every level that we go to in God there is an anointing, a mantle of power, this is not a fleshly act, nor will it ever line up with our flesh. These levels of power can only be obtained through the Spirit.

Going deeper meant that some things had to be let go of, cut off, plucked out. Some people had to be left behind. It also meant that some things in the Spirit that were new had to be embraced, even if I did not understand them with my finite mind. In order to grow in certain areas of grace, I had to release my spirit man into the hands of the Lord. I had to trust that He knew what was best for me.

My mind had to be changed, transformed and renewed daily. I had to develop a strict diet for praying, fasting, and study of the Word. I had to yield myself in the night watches, for God would visit me between 2:30 to 6:00am. I had to set aside Thursday nights for Him, at present, I give Him Monday Nights. He opened a door for that day change, I had to be willing, obedient, and submissive.

The song, "I come to the Garden", was my anthem. For going deeper took me into some places with God that few understood. It was not until I fully embraced the Holy Ghost in my life that God began to expose me to teachers who had been students of His, they were dedicated field workers who would open up the scriptures to me. Some I would see face to face, I bless God, others I would never see, but because they had submitted and done their homework, I was able to grow by the Spirits lead.

Chapter 7
Going Deeper 2

Philippians 4:8-9 Finally, brethren, whatsoever things are true, whatsoever things are honest, whatsoever things are just, whatsoever things are pure, whatsoever things are lovely, whatsoever things are of good report; if there be any virtue, and if there be any praise, think on these things. Those things, which ye have both learned, and received, and heard, and seen in me, do: and the God of peace shall be with you. KJV

After the mind is transformed and renewed, still much attention must be given to our thought life. There is a battle going on in the mind, or should I say, that the mind is a battlefield. Our thinking faculties must line up with Christs thinking. The above scripture gives us description of the things that should have at the forefront of our minds. I've met Christians in the church whose minds are messed up. It is not always so much in what they say, its in another form of conversation, it is in the way they act. My mother, Ms. Cora, used to say these two things;
> *Birds of a feather flock together
> *Show me who you walk with and I will show
> you who you are.

Neither are biblical, but they are truths. A great man of God once said, "If you spend time with the devil in private, he will make you show out in public!" This may be of another translation or may not sound biblical to you, but, it is truth.

Going deeper 2 let me know that we have to be very careful of the things that we entertain in our private lives. We have to practice the art of separating ourselves.

There are friends and family members that I loved dearly, but in order to stay focused on my journey, I had to separate my self. Certain things said or received into our spirit man through fellow-ship will show up in our actions and our speaking. We find ourselves acting in ways that are not pleasing to the kingdom. We will, oops, slip and say things that don't line up to heavenly language.

Going deeper 2 led me to Prayer that extended from the church-house to my house. It brought me from reading the latest magazine, my daily horoscope, and such like to craving my Bible, or books that would help me to live better. It led me to not wanting to watch just anything on TV to the TV watching me whenever it was on what ever wholesome shows I did want to watch.

It change my appetite for certain clothing selections. Some places I used to didn't mind going to, I had no desire to go to those places once I went deeper.

*Philippians 2:5... 3[Let] nothing [be done] through strife or vainglory; but in lowliness of mind let each esteem other better than themselves. 4Look not every man on his own things, but every man also on the things of others. **5Let this mind be in you, which was also in Christ Jesus:** 6Who, being in the form of God, thought it not robbery to be equal with God: 7But made himself of no reputation, and took upon him the form of a servant, and was made in the likeness of men:*

We've shared the entire passage, for it has blessed us as well as encouraged us. We love it all Philippians 2:3-7. The entire passage has blessed my walk. See, I used to hold grudges. My famous last words were, "And, I could care less how you feel." Lord I want to stop and give a shout right now. "Gllllllllllloooooooorrrrrrrryyyyyy!" God did not strike me down in my foolishness.

He kept this Chocolate Doll Baby. I was mean, selfish, I didn't cuss or use fowl words, which to me is worse, for I had the gift of secular carnal gab. I had a way of telling folk off without using one cuss word, I had a look and a walk, that matched. One day I realized that cussing, carrying grudges, not forgiving, hating, they all carried the same penalty. They were all sin which ended in sickness and ultimately death.

I bless God for my change. The more I got to know Him, the better He made me. I knew the Word, His Holy Scriptures. I just wasn't dedicate, consecrated, committed, or walking in line with the Holy Scriptures. In order for God to use me effectively. I had to be converted, my heart had to be changed along with my mind. I had to be purged, my hands had to be cleansed, my heart needed to be made pure. I was compelled to go deeper.

Chapter 8
Great and Mighty Things
& While I Am Yet Speaking

JER33.2 Thus saith the LORD the maker thereof, the LORD that formed it, to establish it; the LORD is his name;
JER33.3 Call unto me, and I will answer thee, and shew thee great and mighty things, which thou knowest not. The Holy Bible, King James Version (KJV)

Heaven declares that if we call unto the Lord, He will answer and show us great and mighty things that we know not of. Once His will becomes clear to us, and we yield ourselves to Him, and began to fervently pray, God will show us great and mighty things.

Every inventor or developer has had this experience. Somewhere, somehow, they had the opportunity for their yielded-desire to meet the divine-will of God, thus we have something great, something new. Every day a new invention is birthed. A new formula, recipe, or revelation is released. Now, some won't give an ounce of the credit to God. Well, that's them. There are some of us who know where all of our help come from.

I read a testimony sharing from my son on face-book today. He is a personal trainer at a Gym in Washington, D.C. He has always been health consience, highly recommending proper exercise, positive thinking, and healthy eating habits. He shared that as he went in to work on today that a lady ran up to him – conversation/fb;

> I walk into Custom Fitness this morning and a
> woman rushes over to me with a big smile and
> says "Are you the man who makes pain go away?
> My sister talks about you all the time."

Of course that blew up his ego for a second, and plus
people started commenting on his stat. But I love a
response that he made to one; his response – comment/fb;

> I've always understood the importance movement
> being progressive and pain-free. Even when I
> didn't have as many tools at my grasp, I had an
> idea.

I admired that response greatly, not just because he is my
child, my first born prince, but the words he chose. I
admit that his response was a gifting that he possesses.
We will further say that he has ears to hear. If we who are
spiritual will develop this mindset, there is no good thing
that God will with-hold from us. We must cast down all
evil imaginations that exalt itself against God, and adhere
to His directing. His teaching, His lead, His instructions,
His guide is the idea that we have. We could have not
thought of it, if it had not been for Him.

Even in our prayer life....the scripture says... *Likewise the
Spirit also helpeth our infirmities: for we know not what we should
pray for as we ought: but the Spirit itself maketh intercession for
us with groanings which cannot be uttered. And he that searcheth
the hearts knoweth what is the mind of the Spirit, because he
maketh intercession for the saints according to the will of God.
And we know that all things work together for good to them that
love God, to them who are the called according to his purpose.
Romans 8:26-28, (KJV)*

We readily testify to the latter. We love Him and we know
that we are called for His purpose. Well, take the whole
roll, and embrace our Help.

The Spirit helps us, He makes intercession for us. He search our hearts. He knows what is within the mind of the Spirit within each one of us. He intercedes for His will and way to be made plain in our lives as we receive the promise of all things work together for our good. Even when things don't work according to our plans. Even when results sound wrong, smell wrong, look wrong, taste wrong, etc. We have got to know that all things are working out for our good. This is why it is imperative that we pray and be willing to receive the answers to our prayers according to His will and not our way.

One thing that we believe is that as we offer prayer in His will, when our desire meet His will, answers for our praying comes forth. If at any time when we pray and are upset or disturbed at the answer, we have not prayed in His will. For praying His will, His way will condition us for His answer. We will understand that God's will for us for that prayer may be different from what we've desired.

One of the hardest lessons for me to learn on this walk was that sometimes we can have faith for that which we don't need. God spoke to me once and said, just because you have faith for it does not mean you are ready for it. If it seems that when we pray for a thing, and when it come to pass we are overwhelmed. Well, I had to learn that, *The blessings of the Lord maketh rich and He addeth no sorrow with it (Proverbs 10:22)*. Of course it was some years ago, but I learned to consult Him for His will, before passing out, bumping my head against the wall, and kicking my feet about what I needed. I now say, if it be Your will Lord. There is never a struggle to hold on to that which He blesses us with. Sometimes our children will cry and cry for something, lets just say ice cream or cookies.

After so long we will give-in and give it to them, knowing that they don't need it. And when we do, they develop a bad tummy ache, they wanted it, they asked for it, we gave it to them, now they are sick, and we feel bad. I believe we serve a merciful, loving, caring God; just as we would do our children, our God continues to care for us the same.

Theres another portion of scripture that I'd like to share right here. Isaiah 65:24 I will answer them before they even call to me.
   While they are still talking about their needs, I will go ahead and answer their prayers! (NLT)

Oh, My God! I Bless You! Actually, the entire 65th Chapter of Isaiah is awesomely power-filled. This passage is a demonstration of the New Heavens and a new earth. The Scriipture text that we have been inspired to use is one of promise. So many times our life experience, during our kingdom walk, we have had the thought to pray for a thing and simontaniously the answer came.

The world does not understand or know of this God-given promise of scripture. One may say that we are practicing witchcraft. But, because we know in whom we believe and serve. And, we have revealed knowledge of this passage of scripture, we can say without a shadow of a doubt, that our God backs His promise.

God made a believer out of me. He proved Himself. When I'd think it, He would manisfest it. Before I could call it, He would bring it. While I would be yet speaking on it, He would release it. Those are times that let me know, that He is real. Sometimes I would sing, "You can't make me doubt Him, I know too much about Him, You can't make me doubt Him in my heart." You see, He's in my heart. **42**

Chapter 9
Weapons

WEAPON – Any implement for fighting or warfare. In the Kingdom, it is not carnal, but mighty through God for the pulling down of stronghold. (2015/From the Prayer Warriors and Intercessors Handbook, Ambassador Black)

No weapon formed against thee shall prosper; and every tongue that shall rise against thee in judgment thou shalt condemn. This is the heritage of the servants of the LORD, and their righteousness is of me, saith the LORD. Isaiah 54:17 (KJV)

In this passage the word weapon refers to foolish talking and jesting,rash and vain swearing, evil-speaking – in general, and slander. It includes lying, hypocritical speaking. It also cover accusations made by Satan of the brethren.

I admit during my childhood, I had what we call, thin skin. My feelings were easy to get hurt, especially when people said ugly things to me. If I was being picked on or talked about, and when I was lied on. I always believed that children could be cruel. I soon found out that grown folk, especially church folk, could be worse.

Once grown, many issues began when I said, I totally commit my ways unto the Lord. I began having episodes of low self esteem and depression. I'd have anxiety attacks. By the time I was age 26, I had a major stroke and was paralyzed from my waist down. I had to learn to walk again. At the same time, I'd given birth to a

43

gorgeous baby boy who was to die and not live through his first night hear on earth. He was born with Strept Throat and pneumonia. Also, a new demon sought to attack me, the spirit of detachment, because I had been separated from my parents as a child, I suffered from a spirit of lonliness as a result of the separation. All of this happened to me from age 16 to 26, ten years, but my God was faithful. And I was determined,

Thus a new chapter opened in my life where I had to re-define weapons. For all of these incidences I learned were attacks formed against my life, that were designed to make me stop and give up. After this ten year interval, I re-didicated my life to the Lord. Trusting totally in Him, giving my life over, has prooved to be the best arrangement that I have ever made. I had found my savior, and I declared that I would not turn back.

My son Donnell was born in 1983, by 1985 I gave birth to my only daughter. The year was 1989. I had been cata-palted deep enough into church by God, and now wondered was this a place where I really wanted to be. My assignment was to work in the kitchen, our choir was selling dinners. Everything was going smoothly we were at the end of the event and an argument was sparked over some stuffing. Me, I was like, what in the world, I never saw anyone fight over food. You see, my mom made dressing often, it went like mac-n-cheese, rice, or mashed potatoes, it was a regular side dish.

Once the arguing and name calling started, I was ready to jump ship. The disagreement was between a sister and a brother from the choir. He began to bring out what one would call old hash about people being unsaved and long as she had been saved, she and people like her who were

44

still new members and should stay with te new members and not with the saints that had seniority.

He began to go on and on about the lifestyle of new members. My feelings were about to be hurt. I had been in the choir long enough to have a few friends, plus I had a half-sister who was in the auxiliary as well. I began to shake, and got really nervous, because this was all new to me. A few friends and sainted sisters came over as they were calling some of the leaders over the choir to come and break up the fight.

Me, I wanted to go back to Nickerson Gardens Housing Projects, where I could watch real fights between the gang bangers, the Bounty Hunters and Crips gangs. That day I realized that there was real fights in the church. Two forms of arsenal was used in the kitchen that day. There was crazy talk, name calling and there were hands, pushing, shoving and even a slap or two. Through all of that though I learned, that the weapons of our warfare is not carnal.

What was carnal? All of it, the crazy talk, name calling and the physical slapping and shoving. The weapons that had been formed was more words against each other, than the actual fight. Being a new member, I felt very offended, uncomfortable and unwanted. Another thing was that all of what the brother had said was not just toward the sister, but toward all of us in the kitchen as well, for at the time there were a few of us new members in the kitchen. I knew deep down inside that none of it was true and it did not apply to me. After I went home, I relished over the prayers that had been made which cause peace to come to that broken situation. It was a Saturday afternoon. I laid across my bed, and kept shaking my head, saying to my self, I don't know if I want to be part of this.

That Sunday morning, I rose early, dressed my kids and myself and made my way to Greater Bethany Community Church. I was ready to march in with the choir at 10:45am. I came to the conclusion that the fight was NOT my fight. The words, even though they had been spoken out loud, in my presence were NOT for me. Yes, the words had been formed, they fit my category, for I was a New Member, but they did not fit my character.

Since that encounter I have found myself voicing that line a many times...That's not my trial, or that's not my fight. For situations come and go, but we need to understand, what is meant for us and whats not. Every issue is not our issue. There are personal battles, then there are those that we may be in the vicinity of, but not directly involve us.

1John 4.4 Ye are of God, little children, and have overcome them: **because greater is he that is in you, than he that is in the world.** *(KJV)* . Psalmist, Sister JoAnn Whatley would testify during service time a portion of our main text scripture above along with the bold portion of this scripture, it went like this.

"Greater is He that is in me than he that is in the world!----
Soooooo, No weapon formed against me, my family, my friends,
my job shall prosper --- Whhhhhyyyy, because greater is He, who
is in me than he that is in the world....Annnnnd, for that reason,
No weapon, formed against me, my family, my friends, my
children, my job shall prosper, causssssseee, greater, I said greater,
I said greater is He, that is in me, than he that is in the world.
Halleluah, Halleluah, Halleluah!!!!

I embraced her testimony and overcame. Now I can look back on that experience and just smile in the Holy Ghost.

Chapter 10
My Recommendation of Personal CPR

1 Thessalonians 5:16-23
The Seven Step Program with a Promise

Step #1 - 16 Rejoice evermore.
Step #2 - 17 Pray without ceasing.
Step #3 - 18 In every thing give thanks: for this is the will of God in Christ Jesus concerning you.
Step #4 - 19 Quench not the Spirit.
Step #5 - 20 Despise not prophesyings.
Step #6 - 21 Prove all things; hold fast that which is good.
Step #7 - 22 Abstain from all appearance of evil.
The Promise - 23 And the very God of peace sanctify you wholly; and I pray God your whole spirit and soul and body be preserved blameless unto the coming of our Lord Jesus Christ.

Cardiopulmonary resuscitation, commonly known as **CPR**,[1] is an emergency procedure performed in an effort to manually preserve intact brain function until further measures are taken to restore spontaneous blood circulation and breathing in a person who is in cadiac arrest. It is indicated in those who are unresponsive with no breathing or abnormal breathing, for example, agonal respirations. (Wikepedia)

CPR is used in the natural sense when one is out of breath or pulled from a near death experience, such as drowning. Spiritual CPR is necessary when our hearts have been so far removed from the things of God that we appear spiritually dead. His Spirit lies dormant in our lives as our walk demonstrates a need for our reviving. We are in a state of denial, and don't realize that we ourselves need help until we allow the Spirit of the living God to nudge us or we feel a trickle effect that something is seriously wrong, we have hit bottom, and we need God to **resuscitate** us. We are on the verge of becoming walking supucles or in a back-slidden state.

In most cases, ours senses and rationale has become distorted. Dull and lifeless-ness has set in. Prayer is not being made. We are not as sensitive to the Spirit of God. Souls have become fragmented. It is a door opener to a schizophrenia. These are times when we need the Holy Ghost Himself to apply the Blood of Jesus to our circumstance. We need the Him to perform CPR on us, we need to get with someone who is strong, and have them to call on Jesus with us and on our behalf.

I learned that there is no harm in dancing off of someone elses testimony. I learned that there may be someone that my God had on assignment, standing watch, that could help me get my prayer through. I found out that the formula of two or more, touching and agreeing wasn't just for weak folk, but for folk that had heard the voice of the Lord saying that He would come and be in the midst.

I found out that if I rejoiced with them that rejoiced, prayed with them that prayed, trusted with them that trusted in the Lord, that I was in pretty good company. If I hung around spiritual people, they would rub off on me, and I became more spiritual. The more they talked about the Word of God and lived Holy, the more my desire was captivated and my appetite began to change. It didn't happen over night. But, before long I wanted to talk about the Word, I developed a longing to live Holy. I came along way from that kitchen scene, to saying, "I'm gonna be sanctified, Holy, my body, my soul, and my spirit, and God said, that He, Himself will find me blameless until He comes."

I receive that promise, and I expect to have it in the end.

Chapter 11
Personal Examples - Women of Silence

God gave to me two Conferences that would celebrate the women. First, Women of Silence which profiled women in scripture who were pray-ers. The other one conference was the Women of Fire.

These women were prolific for their season in that both their prayers and their actions affected the people of their time with change. Who were these women, they were brave and self sacrificing women who were chosen for their time. I will share the Biblical Profile of at least four that were celebrated in these conferences.

The selected women prayed in quiet times, dangerous times, and exciting times. At the Conferences churches would come together, Saints from ages 0-99, men, women, girls and boys. And we would celebrate the lessons learned from the women in profile.

I confess, I've always been inspired by women who are real firebrands. They seem quiet, like they don't know or care about whats going on around them. I had the privilege of connecting with some in the earth realm. I will list some in the back of the book. We often refer to the scriptures for our biblical witnesses,

One – Queen Esther –
Theme, "For Such A Time As This"

I was both encouraged and impressed by Queen Esther

whose name mean Myrtle, as in the tree. She rose from being an orphan to marrying the King. She was raised by her uncle, Mordecai. She was groomed and prepared to walk as one of the virgins who had the assignment to be in positionthe King to choose from. She faced her adversaries well. The prophetic Word for her season was found in Chapter 4:14.

For if thou altogether holdest thy peace at this time, then shall there enlargement and deliverane arise to the Jews from another place; but thou and thy father's house shall be destroyed: and who knoweth whether thou art come into the kingdom for such a time as this? Esther 4:14 KJV

In her silence she had to cry our in order for deliverance to come for the King and her people. There is an Esther anointing that will flow in the life of todays chosen and selected woman. Esther deveoped skill, tact, and clout in a short period of time, we should desire this favor on our lives today, as women on a mission for the deliverance of those who are held in bondage. Esther was a Kingdom mover – she was anointed to be a Kingdom Shaker.

Two – Jael - The theme for that Conference was, "Got Milk!"

*Right Can Defeat Might...*Jael's story is similar to the story of David and Goliath.Though she was a weak woman, Jael triumphed over a seemingly invincible warrior, Sisera. The story ridiculed the Canaanite warriors: being murdered by a weak woman was a shameful way for a soldier to die. It was also shameful for their leaders, who had been 'stung' by a holy woman.

To drive the point home, there was a humiliating element

of sexual derision in the story: male sexual symbols such as the hammer and nails were used, but by a woman against a man. Sisera, the victim fled from Deborah (Judges 4:12-16, 5:19-23) tricked the over-confident enemy into driving their iron-wheeled chariots onto marshy land where they were bogged down.
Then the Israelite slingsmen and archers picked them off one by one.

the enemy forces were routed, their troop slaughtered, and the Israelites were jubilant. Sisera, the enemy general, fled from the battlefield towards the encampment of Jael the Kenite.

Jael met Sisera and killed him (Judges 4:17-24, 5:24-27) *The woman who was profiled for the Conference, Jael,* used a tent peg and mallet to kill the unwary enemy general, Sisera. She called Sisera into her tent, hid him and fed him.

JUD4.17 Howbeit Sisera fled away on his feet to the tent of Jael the wife of Heber the Kenite: for there was peace between Jabin the king of Hazor and the house of Heber the Kenite. JUD4.18 And Jael went out to meet Sisera, and said unto him, Turn in, my lord, turn in to me; fear not. And when he had turned in unto her into the tent, she covered him with a mantle. **JUD4.19 And he said unto her, Give me, I pray thee, a little water to drink; for I am thirsty. And she opened a bottle of milk, and gave him drink, and covered him.** *KJV*

After he fell into exhausted sleep she drove a tent peg through the side of his head. She was hailed as a national heroine by the pursuing Israelite forces led by Deborah and Barak.   **53**

I declare milk has an anointing upon it to slay the enemy. So, even in a New Convert stage, if all you have is the Milk of the Word, or if thats all you can think of, use what you have. God will bless it, increase it and bring you to victory. Little becomes much when placed in the Masters Hand.

Number Three - Hagar –
Theme: "The Cry of a Thirsty Woman."

The story of Hagar is one that is hard for us to understand in our culture today; she certainly was a victim of circumstances. As Sarah's maid servant, or slave, she did not have a say in the circumstances of her life--even when it involved bearing children for her mistress!

So many times in life, we have the experience of being a victim of circumstances. Life comes with all sorts of activities of daily living. Some good, some bad, but most certainly, if we keep our focus on the Lord while going through, He will bring us out everytime.

When it seems like we are at our wits end, about to throw in the towel, when it seems like, the odds are against us, God will bring us through. I believe the Bible says that when the enemy (or life) comes against us like a flood, the Lord will lift up a standard, in other words, He will work it out for our good.

Now, Abram named his son, whom Hagar bore, Ishmael. Genesis 16:15

Therefore she [Sarah] said to Abraham, "Cast out this bondwoman and her son; for the son of this bondwoman shall not be heir with my son, namely with Isaac."
Genesis 21:10

So Abraham rose early in the morning, and took bread and a skin of his mother, and sent her away. Then she departed and wandered in the Wilderness of Beersheba.
Genesis 21:14, New King James Version

God had long promised to Abraham that He would bless him with seed as the stars in heaven and the sand upon the seashore. As he and Sarah grew older, it became obvious that this seed was not going to come through Sarah. At least, that was Sarah's assessment of the situation. After thinking through the dilema, she developed an alternate solution. Sarah would use her maid servant; if she gave her to Abraham to be impregnated by him, the child would really belong to Sarah. Therefore Abraham would have descendants through Abraham and Sarah, via her "proxy".

Ishmael, as the son of Sarah's maid servant and Abraham, was never considered Sarah's son by God. His promise was to Abraham and Sarah. After Sarah was past childbearing age, God miraculously fulfilled his promise to Abraham when Sarah gave birth to Isaac. From this point on, Ishmael became an antagonist of Isaac. When Isaac reached the age of 13, Sarah could no longer tolerate the situation and demanded that her maid servant and Ishmael be sent away. After consulting God, Abraham discovered that this came about by the intentions of God and that God would protect Ishmael and make a nation out of him as well.

In Genesis 41:14 we read that Ishmael and his mother were given supplies and sent away. At this point, let's step back a little and think about Hagar. None of this had come about by her will; as a slave she was acting upon commands imposed upon her. Now she finds herself cast away: she became the discarded wife. She and Ishmael are sent away to wander in the desert; left to die. If one would have cause to be bitter about life, this would certainly be it. God, however, appeared to her in the desert and assured her of His protection and of his plans for Ishmael. From this point on, we are no longer told anything about Hagar's life. We do know from history that God did, indeed, fulfill all of His promises. The Arab nations are direct descendants from Ishmael.

Do you wonder at the constant strife between the nation of Israel and the Arab nations? Do you really think the strife is due to oil or money? Why do they still fight over a small portion of land, each claiming rightful ownership? Today, we have learned the root of that strife; the contention between Sarah and her mistress and between Isaac and Ishmael continues to this day, and always will until the Lord returns.

God sends us many difficult situations, but rarely as difficult as Hagar's. Even so, His grace was there for her;

His protection was upon her.It is good for us to step back occasionaly and realize that we are all a part of a bigger picture. God has a plan for this world, and He will bring it to pass. From Biblical history we discover that He often used simple or lowly people such as in this lowly maid servant. Do not underestimate your own importance in God's plan; no one is ever too small for God to use. Everything that happens in your life is ordained by God and is a part of His greater plan for this earth.

Alone in the desert, Hagar and Ishmael soon used up their tiny supply of water. Hagar searched desperately for more but found none, and saw her son begin to die of thirst.

GEN21.16 And she went, and sat her down over against him a good way off, as it were a bow shot: for she said, Let me not see

*the death of the child. And she sat over against him, **and lift up**
her voice, and wept. GEN21.17 **And God heard the voice of the**
lad; and the angel of God called to Hagar out of heaven, and said
unto her, What aileth thee, Hagar? fear not; for God hath heard
the voice of the lad where he is. GEN21.18 Arise, lift up the lad,
and hold him in thine hand; for I will make him a great nation.
GEN21.19 And God opened her eyes, and she saw a well of
water; and she went, and filled the bottle with water, and gave
the lad drink. **Then she drank the water herself.** KJV*

Number Four – Dorcas-
Raised and Empowered to Serve!

The story of Dorcas in the Bible encouraged and inspired me as it reminded me of God's great love for all of
His people. Dorcas was not a great pastor, prophet, or
evangelist, but rather just a plain, everyday person like
you and I. However, she was not too unimportant for God
to include the story of her good works and charitable
deeds in His Holy Word.

I identified with her in that she was a seamstress, and
purple was I would assume her favorable collor. She was
a flexable worker, for the Bible says that she was she was
full of good works and charitable deeds. In other words
she was missionary minded, and this has also been said of
me many times. I happen to have the attitude of whatever
my hands find to do, do it, and do it well.

Now about Tabitha, at Joppa there was a certain disciple
named Tabitha, which is translated Dorcas. This woman
was full of good works and charitable deeds which she
did. But it happened in those days that she became sick
and died. When they had washed her, they laid her in an
upper room. And since Lydda was near Joppa, and the disciples had heard that Peter was there, they sent two men to
him, imploring him not to delay in coming to them. Then

Peter arose and went with them. When he had come, they brought him to the upper room. And all the widows stood by him weeping, showing the tunics and garments which Dorcas had made while she was with them. But Peter put them all out, and knelt down and prayed. And turning to the body he said, "Tabitah, arise." And she opened her eyes, and she saw Peter she sat up. Then he gave her his hand and lifted her up; and when he had called the saints and widows, he presented her alive. And it became known throughout all Joppa, and many believed on the Lord.

36There was a believer in Joppa named Tabitha (which in Greek is Dorcas*). She was always doing kind things for others and helping the poor. 37About this time she became ill and died. Her body was washed for burial and laid in an upstairs room. 38But the believers had heard that Peter was nearby at Lydda, so they sent two men to beg him, "Please come as soon as possible!" 39So Peter returned with them; and as soon as he arrived, they took him to the upstairs room. The room was filled with widows who were weeping and showing him the coats and other clothes Dorcas had made for them. 40But Peter asked them all to leave the room; then he knelt and prayed. Turning to the body he said, "Get up, Tabitha." And she opened her eyes! When she saw Peter, she sat up! 41He gave her his hand and helped her up. Then he called in the widows and all the believers, and he presented her to them alive 42The news spread through the whole town, and many believed in the Lord. Acts 9:36-42 (NLT)

Chapter 13
From Prayer Warrior to Prophetic Intercession

I had an awesome, awesome, awesome prayer room experience with those Missionary Warriors of the upper room at Greater Bethany Community Church in the late eighties. But then, the Lord saw fit to advance me in His Kingdom. He moved me from California to Mississippi.

When He did so, He connected me with some more Missionary Warriors. Just when I thought that I had arrived, He dropped this bombshell of a term on me. He said to me that I was a Prophetic Intercessor. I said o.k., the year was 1994.

A Prophetic intercessor is one who prays a very sharp and powerful prayer that is communicated as a prophetic word. This is different than asking the Lord to do something, which would be a prayer of petition. Instead, it commands something to be done and puts the invisible realm into motion to bring it to pass. God respects this type of prayer as it reflects who He is. He is the Word and everything came into existence because He spoke it out.

With Heaven in my view, and this new mandate in my life on my way to my destiny. I literally had to look into the face of God, and say Lord okay, you mean I am to speak in prayer the things that are on Your heart and You will hear me and bring them to pass. This was before I had been exposed to terms like, decree and declare. One thing I have learned about God is that He teaches us a little along. He won't drop everything on us at once. He gives us a little at a time.

He gives it in His timing, as we are able to digest it. He will not give us meat when we need to be on milk. He ultimately blesses us according to our ability to accept in every area of our lives. He deals with each of us bountifully in His own way. He knows each and every one of us, He made us, He knows each hair on our heads, the old saints used to say. He knows everything about you and I. Everything. He is an all-seeing, all-knowing – He is Omniscient, Omnipotent, Omnipresent, He is everywhere, He is everything at the same time.

Someone once said, He is all powerful. Oh yes, I found Him to be all that in my life and more. I found out that if I would just trust Him, open my mouth wide, (Psalms 81:10), that He would fill it. Fill it with prayers, fill it with those things that I was to speak and pray about. You see, He already knows our needs, He just wants to know if He can trust us long enough, that we will knock, seek, and ask not for our sake, but on behalf of others.

The scripture Ezekiel 22:30 the Lord says this, *The people of the land have used oppression, and exercised robbery, and have vexed the poor and needy: yea, they have oppressed the stranger wrongfully. And I sought for a man among them, that should make up the hedge, and stand in the gap before me for the land, that I should not destroy it: but I found none.*

The drop of this scripture came at the beginning of a new season, a new level of prayer for me. I well understood this searching of the Lord. I embraced the burden that He had for the people, and what they were going through. I thought seriously about how the Lord was searching for all the way from ten to one for someone who would intercede, speak to Him concerning the delema of a people.

I looked around in my own city and we were somewhat experiencing the same types of situations. I sensed that there was a call for men and women of God to come and speak on behalf of others, There were things that were to come, and transpire in the lives of those of us in the church. And, God needed us, He was searching for someone to come forth and stand in the gap, make up the hedge, so to speak.

I always believed that this type of assignment was to be re-birthed heavily in the church. God was looking for one who would be sensitive to His burden and cry out in intercession for the people in the city, those that would bombard heavenon their behalf. He searched amongst the people and could find not one to share His burden of prayer. That was an understatement compared to one made by a mentor and friend of mine who says, "Today's Prayer Meetings don't get enough takers to eat a fried chicken!" Of course this was stated in the '90's. Surely, things have changed since then. Ultimately, we both agree that regular attendance and participation to Prayer meetings should be of utmost importance to Choir Members, Praise Team and Dancers, Preachers, Prophets, Trustees, Pastors, Bishops, Apostles, etc...

When one feel as though they should have part in the program or moving of the service, then they should feel obligated to spend time in a structured Prayer Meeting. Today, in the year 2015, a large majority of our Prayer Meetings are held on the phones (tele or cell). There is in todays language what is called a Conference Call. It's just a modernized Prayer Line, which is up-grade from the 80's. The difference between the prayerline and the collective prayer in the House of God is that once God has recruited us and we have accepted the call to be in

Prayer, we must recognize His mandate to have us to meet in the house of God. Not just at home on our telephones. Our awesome God lets us know that He will honor perpetual prayer that is made in His sanctified house.

2 Chronicles 7
14 If my people, which are called by my name, shall humble themselves, and pray, and seek my face, and turn from their wicked ways; then will I hear from heaven, and will forgive their sin, and will heal their land.
15 Now mine eyes shall be open, and mine ears attent unto the prayer that is made in this place.
16 For now have I chosen and sanctified this house, that my name may be there for ever: and mine eyes and mine heart shall be there perpetually.

If I may, allow me to pen right here to the seasoned warriors that God honors prayer that comes from a repentant, humbled, set apart and consecrated heart. Especially those who are called by His Name. I love the portion of that scripture that says, "turn from their wicked ways." I found out one day while reading the Word of God that Christians can be wicked, mean, deceitful, carnal minded, as well as ignorant and unlearned. We can walk with all of these attributes, and think we are alright. But, in actuality, we have much land that needs a healing to take place.

We must seek God's face, secondly, I found out that this was a high order of praying. You see, when we seek His face, we are not just offering up low-level prayers. This is the level of praying where we stand toe to toe with the Spirit of the living God. We are breast to breast to the point of breath to breath, we are in His face.

I found that being in His face brought on a new level of

62

authority. It meant that I was praying distinctly so that Heaven could be shaken. It would send a shaking through the atmosphere that would get God's immediate attention. For in the scripture He says, "*...then will I hear from heaven, and will forgive their sin, and will heal their land. Now mine eyes shall be open, and mine ears attent unto the prayer that is made in this place.*" (a portion of verse 14 and 15)

There is a place in God, where there is a continual life giving flow erupting like none other. It is a safe place. A Holy place. A place of unquestionable authority. This place is where one prays from, effectively, fervently, this is not a place for gainsayers, people of doubt. This is an altar where He says, His eyes are opened, His ears attent unto the Prayer that are going forth in this place.God meets us in this place. I have found that once we meet God faithfully at the Altar, we can meet anyone else, anywhere. Once we develop a divine connection with God at His designated place of meeting, God will enable us to resurrect altars in our own lives. God wants to hear from us, His people, the sheep of His pasture.

In the last verse of 2nd Chronicles 7:14 of our text for this chapter as we close this portion of *For now have I chosen and sanctified this house, that my name may be there for ever: and mine eyes and mine heart shall be there perpetually.*

My God speaks distinctly and profoundly as He makes the statement that He has chosen and sanctified this house. What house, is He referring to the House of God or our temple. I declare a mystery. I say both. His name shall be with us and his eyes and his heart also, perpetually. Meaning forever and ever. He is just that awesome.

This sealed a promise in my spirit man, for deep within me, I had the surety that My God would never leave me nor forsake me. My second unction was that my prayer life was about to take off, I would need some extra tight spiritual seat belts. For we would move swiftly. I could feel it my spirit, and I was reminded of how I had begun to dance in prayer. God was elevating me to a place in Him, that when I'd speak a thing, He would hear me and bring it to pass.

I was at a crossover point, as the Prophet Jeremiah rung into-my spirit, I could hear these words, *"call unto me, and I will answer thee, and shew the great and mighty things, which thou knowest not"*. (Jeremiah 33:3) Another proclamation came to me from the Prophet Isaiah, saying, *"And it shall come to pass, that before they call, I will answer , and while they are yet speaking, I will hear"* (Isaiah 65:24) From the mouths of the Prophets came these two pivoting proclamations that changed a direction for me in the prayer realm.

This let me know that – if I called out in prayer to Him, that He would answer me and show me great and mighty things, that only He knew annnnddd now I can speak it and He would bring it to pass. And even before I speak it He would answer annnnnddd while I would be speaking it forth from my mouth, He would hear. This was Prophetic Intercession, while I would be praying, He would hear me, and answer me and bring it to pass. He gave me the ability in prayer to speak forth things that were dear to His heart,utterances that were to come, that would be revealed and manifest. To a bonifide pray-er, one of the most precious moments is to hear directly from God the directives concerning his or her God-given assignments.

On my face, God showed me the enormousy and immensity of His vastness. There was a deepness in Him that I had to go to in order to be where I needed to be. Thus, I began to write Victory Plans. The year was 2007, the last year that I would chair the State Missionary and Christian Womens Auxiliary Convention for Mississippi and Western Tennesee District Council, PAW, Inc. I was always somewhat saddened, when change came to my life, as I still somewhat suffered with the spirit of detachment. Even as an adult, I suffered from what the world calls separation anxiety. These were Glory Preparation days – but, may I remind us that through it all that God was with me.

God was elevating me from Prayer Warrior to Prophetic Intercessor. He was teaching me to add to my warring and petitioning the art of speaking out those things in prayer. Calling out declarations, declaring and decreeing, instead of asking, speaking that it be done according to His divine will. I believe a confirmation of that comes in the Word of God.

(As it is written, I have made thee a father of many nations,) before him whom he believed, even God, who quickeneth the dead, and calleth those things which be not as though they were. Romans 4:17 - He would give to the Prophetic Intercessor the ability to speak concerning dead situations. Our willingness and obedience to speak would cause life to flow, to be recovered, restored, and repaired to lifeless-ness in any capacity. For His Glory to be revealed. He gave us this charge, along with a Mantle of (His) power and authority.

Chapter 14
THE VICTORY PLAN

Prayer and fasting is a powerful tool to a Bible tool to a Bible toting believer. This has been a designated place that infuses us with power from on high.

In order to walk fully equipped with the necessary power and authority, one must discipline self. One must adhere to a strong diet of the Word of God, prayer, and acts of dedication and commitment. Especially, if there is a desire to see change take place in ones life.

Allow me to share a testimony; We must realize that whatever is going on with us in the natural usually reflects what God is doing in the Spirit. Once this concept is grasped, we will have a better understanding of why things happen and how we should react when they happen.

When God gave me my own personal victory plan, I was going through a hurricane in my life. My body was going through, my children, my job, yet, I had this strategic assignment before me. One thing I learned to do well was to ask God to helpt me to meet Him at this point in my life with all of the chaos.

He spoke to me concerning a victory plan. This plan consisted of Prayer, Bible Reading, and an eating schedule. It has worked so well for me through the years that upon His permission, I shared it wirh others. I'd get pen and paper in hand, and He'd give me divine instructions, I'd follow them, and He would be pleased with the results that came forth. It appeared, the harder the assignments, the more chaos I'd have to deal with.

There were some rule nuggets that the Lord shared with me. Through the years the list has grown, I'm going to share about five of them, they are just something to think on, meditate, then live by.

1. Don't take anything personal on this journey and don't allow anything to intimidate you.
2. When fasting, remember that we are concecerating ourselves to meet Him not people.
3. Trials and tribulations don't come to destroy, they come to distract. We are to learn from them and move on.
4. When pleasing Him on the fast don't try to show out, and fool around and fall out.
5. There are things that may be of utmost importance to me, but not of important to God.

Although fasting is designed to make us humble, powerful, and strong all at the same time. It should not be a burden. We should not be drudgey, pale faced, mean, dry, none-of-that. We should have the testimony of Daniel. When God tells us of a food or activity that we should either apply or refrain from, we should do so with great honor. Being privileged to go through in order to meet our Savior.

My God and I have had some good times. God usually take me for a few days, weeks, months or by the year. I remember one time doing Noodles – Top Ramen, for 31 days, I did not get sick at all. Once, the Lord had me to refrain from Chocolate.

I did well, by the end of the second week I was suffering from chocolate withdrawals.

You God made us in His image, in His image He made us. He knows all about us, so if we are to practice the art of integrity with anyone, It mayest well be Him.

When doing a church call fast by our leaders we must be obedient. If there is an issue with obeying those directives, then off to the leader (I) go. I have not always been heard, and when not I did the best I could to meet the given fast. On a personal level though, when it was God and I, perhaps when I needed to connect with Him, God would speak to me concerning what I needed to do to meet Him.

***One season, He instructed me to eat chicken, fish, and turkey for three months and sometimes up to a year.
***One year, there was no soda, no soft drinks, juice and water only. I could eat my meals, but could only have the juice and water.
***One year, there was no chocolate, I thought I was going to die that year, after about three months, My God!
***One year, He instructed me to go with liquids only, on three to five day intervals, whenever convient for Him.
***One year there was the Top Ramen Noodles for dinner for 31 days. God has truly been good.
***One year, there was salad and vegetables for a year. I could eat a meal on Sunday, my meat was fish, chicken or turkey.
***One season, it was fruit for seven days, Salad for seven days, Fruit then back on salad. God was faithful!!! Only drinking water, tea, and juice.

Someone may say, that I was eating, thats when I say Not what I wanted, but the fast that God had released me to eat.

From time to time different people of influence will receive revelation on a fast that God has has given to them. We don't view this as neither here nor there, for any revelation from God is to be regarded as divine impartaion.

What is to be considered is – Is this the plan for me, and how will God get the Glory out of this. Will God be pleased with me for my efforts in this. Fasting is a vehicle that we use combined with pray that enables us with the power that is needed to effectively Minister.

Jesus shares with us disciples Matthew 17:21 and Mark 9:29, *This kind can come out only by prayer and fasting* (NET) The disciples had met with a spirit that they could not cast out. So Jesus had to advise them of why they were not effective then gave them a formula of how it could get done.

When we fast, abstain and concecrate ourselves for ministry, it is for God's glory and not our own. We have no glory, all glory belong to God. People fast for various reason. Some being far from obtaining the power of God.

I love the Victory Plans that God gave me to execute in my life and I want to encourage you in it works, yes it work. Through the years plans have changed from person to person, denomination to demonination, movement to movement. This is why we admonish you – the faster – to listen to your leader, your physician, as well as praying to God to see what will be required in order to meet Him.

VICTORY PLAN
Spiritual Housekeeping

There are several plans that I have written over the years. This one I find most effective in that it takes care of both the flesh and the spirit. Once these areas are covered, disciplined, and fully dealt with, we will flow in the kingdom being effective and operate in a spirit of excelllency. I pray that this plan will work as well for you, my dear readers, as it has worked for me.

After God has given the Eating Plan, it's best to stock the items He gives. Mainly because I don't like running out of stuff, nor do I like substiting items, for to me that would be altering the order that was given by the Lord. There is reward for the discipline in keeping order with the plan that's giving.

The Shopping List
Please read all labels before purchasing. Do not purchase anything which has refined sugars, excessive salt and/or additives. Also , I strongly suggest that you consult your doctor (especially those on medication) befo re you alter your diet or initiate a fast.

Instructions on meal planning - Select 1 item only from each section to mix and match your meal of choice. Only 3 meals per day for 3 days, then 2 meals per day for 3 days and repeat.

MEATS
Chicken, Fish or Turkey (Small 1 ½ cup servings – 1 per day)

VEGETABLES

Avocados (avoid for weight loss), Leeks, Carrots, Yams, Bean Sprouts, Cabbage, Broccoli, Radishes, Beets, Peppers, Cucumber, Watercress, Potatoes, Squashes, Plantain, Egg Plant, Celery, Cauliflower, Zucchini, Peas, Turnips, Pumpkin, Brussels Sprouts, Onions, Sweet Potatoes, Parsnips, Artichokes, Asparagus, Tomatoes (limit because of acidity)

SALAD/GREEN LEAFY VEGETABLES

Romaine Lettuce, Chives, Radishes, Watercress, Coriander, Spinach, Swiss Chard, Kale, Spinach Beet, Mixed Swiss Chard, Collard Greens, Cucumber, Celery Spring Mixes, Turnips, collards, Mustards

FRUIT

Apples, Tangerines, Apricots, Grapes, Blackberries, Bananas (not during detox), Cherries, Lemons, Cranberries, Strawberries, Grapefruit, Pears, Plums, Greengages, Guavas, Pineapples, Melons (eat alone), Kiwi Fruit, Peaches, Mangoes, Star Fruit, Limes, Papaya, Currents Cranberries, Gooseberries, Frozen for smoothies or refreshings.

BREADS/CEREAL

Ezekiel (Bread and Pita), Pumpernickel, Sprouted Wheat/grains (unbleached), Rye, Oat, Millet, Quinoa, Tortilla, Buckwheat, bagels, English Muffin, Oat Meal, Grits, Cream-o-wheat, Malt-o-meal, Cold Cereals (non-sugar and do not add sugar, see sweetners)

HERBS/SPICES

Fresh Ginger, Garlic, Onions, Cilantro, Dill, Chives, Bay Leaves, Basil, Coriander, Oregano, Thyme, Parsley, Marjoram, Tarragon, Mint, Rosemary, Sage

LEGUMES/BEANS/SPROUTS
Kidney, Green Navy, Pole, String-beans, Lentil, Chick-pea, Red Beans, PINTO beans, Broad Beans, Wax Beans, Black-eyed, Butter Beans, Lima, Pinto Beans, Haircot Beans, Soy Beans, Alfafa Srouts, Bean Sprouts, Broccoli Sprouts, Green beans, Green Peas

DRIED FRUITS & NUTS (snacks)
Dates, Figs, Prunes, Raisins. *SNACK BAGS* I use mixed dried fruit bags; pineapples, dates, raisins, etc. I usually get 2 or 3 different kinds. Add cashews, pecans or walnuts. Your choice of cereal, Honey Nut Cheerios, Raisin Bran, whole grain. Chocolate covered raisins, peanuts, Sunflower Seeds, Pumpkin Seeds, etc. shake it all up. I snack on it across the day, I eat less at mealtime and have plenty of wholesome snack.

NON-DAIRY/DAIRY
Almond Milk, Soy Milk, Rice Milk, Goats' Cheese, Natural Yogurt, Hummus, Milk 1% or 2%

DRINK LIST
Purified/Distilled Water – Aquafina, Sams' Club or Dasani, they have extra nutrents (8 glasses!!), Pure Water, Aquifina, Herb Teas, Fresh Vegetable Juices, Fresh Fruit Juices, Green Drinks, Hot, Water & Lemon (upon rising)

SWEETNERS Honey, Molasses, Stevia (sugar
alternative), Pepper Jelly, Homemade Jellies or Jams

SEASONING/CONDIMENTS
Miso Tamari Soy Sauce Vegesall Braggs Amino Acid Allspice Cayenne Pepper Cinnamon Ginger Cloves Tofu Spreads Mustard Saffron Sea Salt Turmeric Paprika Balsamic Vinegar/Oil (makes a delicious salad dressing)

Other Natural Herbs and Spices, etc.

SUPPLEMENTS Kelp A Good Multivitamin Olive Leaf
Grape Seed Extract Noni Juice Colloidal Minierals Olive
Oil (1tbs. Twice daily) Oxy-charge (add 7 drops to water
3 times a day)
LIVER TONIC Black Grapes Fresh garlic/Garlic tablets
Pure Carrot/Beet/Celery Juice (3 times per week)
KIDNEY TONIC Cranberry Tablet Supplement Hot
Water/Honey/Braggs Apple Cider Vinegar (sip slowly)
Hot Water/Braggs Apple Cider Vinegar/Cayenne/Honey
(sip slowly)

FOODS TO AVOID
(do not eat!!!) Refined Foods Avocado (those interested in
weight loss) Wheat/Wheat Products Refined Breads
Oranges (too acidic) Caffeine Fried Foods Lentils (during
consecration) Red Meats Chicken Chocolates Mushrooms
(full of fungus) Shell Fish Peanuts Salt Fast Foods
Candy/Cakes/Cookies Spinach (if you are detoxing) Sodas
Carbonated Water Processed Luncheon Meats Dairy
Products/Cow's Milk (full of steroids/growth hormones)
Some juices. *Anything that gases you normally.*

JUICE COMBINATIONS
1. Beet, celery, alfalfa sprouts
2. Cabbage, celery and apple
3. Cabbage, cucumber, celery, tomato, spinach and
    basil
4. Tomato, carrot and mint
5. Carrot, celery, watercress, garlic and wheat-grass
6. Grapefruit, orange, lemon
7. Beet, parsley, celery, carrot, mustard greens, garlic
8. Beet, celery, dulse and carrot
9. Cucumber, carrot, and mint

10. Carrot, celery, parsley, onion, cabbage and sweet basil
11. Carrot and coconut milk
12. Carrot, broccoli, lemon, cayenne
13. Carrot, cauliflower, rosemary
14. Apple, carrot, radish, ginger
15. Apple, pineapple and mint
16. Apple, papaya and grapes
17. Papaya, cranberries and apples
18. Grape, cherry and apple
19. Watermelon (include seeds)
20. Leafy greens, broccoli, apples
21. Beets, celery and carrots
22. Asparagus, carrot, and mint
23. Lemon, strawberry, banana
24. Peanut butter, banana, blueberries
25. Your own favorite combinations

MEATS Baked/broiled/boiled/steamed - Fish, Chicken or Turkey. No fried foods.

WHAT TO EXPECT
As the body throws off/rids itself of toxins you can expect some of the following to occur: Fuzzy/Coated Tongue Headache Irritability Increased Bowel Movements Constipation Change In Skin Tone Nausea Break-outs Change in Body Scent Bad breath

SPIRITUAL MAINTENANCE
Daily Scriptural Reading
Unity Prayer – With the church prayer group.
Journaling Personal Devotions/Prayers/Meditations

NIGHT SNACK Sample: Across the day as often as you like drink Hot Water & Lemon with a drop or two of honey. Melon Warm Soy/Rice/Almond Milk (my favorite is almond milk) Cup of yogurt (frozen or regular), Apple sauce, ½ Peanut butter sandwich so you won't wake up starved.

Drink plenty liquid, choose ones that refreshes you, God will give you what works for you Hot, cold, lukewarm water, honey, lemon and a pinch of cayenne pepper Herb Teas (drink often, maybe throughout the day water & lemon) all non-alcoholic beverages.

WHAT TO EXPECT
As the body throws off/rids itself of toxins you can expect some of the following to occur: Fuzzy/Coated Tongue Headache Irritability Increased Bowel Movements Constipation Change In Skin Tone Nausea Break-outs Change in Body Scent Bad breath

DO'S FOR BODY MAINTENANCE Take Showers or
Baths Twice Daily Dry Skin Brushing With Loofa Brush (exfoliates skin & increases circulation) Self Massage Maintain Peaceful Environment Exercise (brisk walking outdoors) Steam Baths/Sauna (twice weekly) Bath Twice Weekly In Epsom Salts Or Baking Soda (draws out impurities) Use Glycerin or Lemon Soaps if possible. For baths and wash'ups try to use white soaps.

SPIRITUAL MAINTENANCE
Daily Scriptural Reading (see attached calendar) Corporate Prayer – 7:00p.m. nightly Journaling Personal Devotions/Prayers/Meditations Do as much outside sitting as possible.

DAILY PLAN: 12 DAYS - REPEAT ONCE PER MONTH
Throughout the year (144 days)
1)PRAYER FOCUS
2)SCRIPTURE READING
3)STUDY NOTES

DAY 1.2,3

Prayer Focus: Father, I come to you today to begin my victory plan. Lord, I empty out, repenting of any and all things that I have done or said that was not pleasing in your sight. Father, I bless You in advance for meeting me in this plan, trusting that ever crevice, corner, thought, will be analyed and brought to surface, then nipped at the root. Father, I have strayed in unknown ways, I believe You to help me to get back onto the straight and narrow. Purge me Lord, cleanse me through and through. Deliver my tongue from backbiting, Deliver me from slandering and malice. Help me Father to examine myself, show me the check and balance of my own life. Father, help me to see myself, Help me to gain more of how to please you in all of my ways. I praise You now, in Your precious Name. Amen.

Bible Reading: Romans 1:25-32

25 Because they exchanged the truth of God for a lie and worshiped and served the creature rather than the Creator, Who is blessed forever! Amen (so be it). 26 For this reason God gave them over and abandoned them to vile affections and degrading passions. For their women exchanged their natural function for an unnatural and abnormal one, 27 And the men also turned from natural relations with women and were set ablaze (burning out, consumed) with lust for one another—men committing

*shameful acts with men and suffering in their own bodies
and personalities the inevitable consequences and penalty
of their wrong-doing and going astray, which was [their]
fitting retribution. 28 And so, since they did not see fit to
acknowledge God or approve of Him or consider Him
worth the knowing, God gave them over to a base and
condemned mind to do things not proper or decent but
loathsome, 29 Until they were filled (permeated and
saturated) with every kind of unrighteousness, iniquity,
grasping and covetous greed, and malice. [They were] full
of envy and jealousy, murder, strife, deceit and treachery,
ill will and cruel ways. [They were] secret backbiters and
gossipers, 30 Slanderers, hateful to and hating God, full
of insolence, arrogance, [and] boasting; inventors of new
forms of evil, disobedient and undutiful to parents. 31
[They were] without understanding, conscienceless and
faithless, heartless and loveless [and] merciless. 32
Though they are fully aware of God's righteous decree
that those who do such things deserve to die, they not only
do them themselves but approve and applaud others who
practice them. Holy Bible: Amplified*

Study Note: One day I had to look at myself, I had to be
honest with myself. I found out that when I was honest
with myself, that I could be honest with others, and then I
could turn to God, and say, search me Lord. I had to pray
the prayer, Lord, give me the power to see myself, what
am I bringing to the Kingdom for advancement.. In this
particular passage there were two things that stood out.

1. What would happen to me if I gave up truth of
   God and flowed with a lie or a lie.
2. Seeing that God has no respect of person, how
   would He view or measure your sin, and is one sin
   worse than another.

This passage really helped me. Let's take our time and mull over this passage for a period of three days. We will see the line-up of spirits that can overtake us. We have to be very careful lest these things can creep into our lives. Innocent actions are in a line up with lethal ones, check it out. Read the scripture as many times as you get a chance, over the 3 days. Make notes, highlight some wordsundestand., look some words that you don't

Day 4,5,6

Romans 8:1-9

Prayer Focus: Father, I bless You, I thank You for being such a Mighty God. I come again, with a repentant heart, asking You to forgive me for all of my sins committed, known and unknown. Lord, as I continue this consecration, help me to see myself, my ways of error. I thank You for the strenth and wisdom that You have given me. Help me Father to make wise choices not entertaining those things that lead me outside of Your will. Help me to stay on a plainpath. I bless You Lord, for you have let me know that I must seek Your will, Youir face, You have encouraged me in that, if I walk after You I will not fulfill the lust of the flesh. Father, help me to dicern what Spirit is flowing, help me to see Your Spirit, knowing the difference from that of You and that of the flesh. Help me not to be so distracted, with evey wave in wind that comes through. We come against wisdom that is not of You. Help me to see You at every turn. Thank You for helping me not to walk with a spirit of condemnation I thank You for being a lamp unto my feet and a light unto my path. Show me how to walk fully after Your Spirit, dedicatd for and in Your service. Amen.

Bible Reading: Romans 8:1-10 *1 THEREFORE, [there is] now condemnation (no adjudging guilty of wrong) for those who are in Christ Jesus, who live [and] walk not after the dictates of the flesh, but after the dictates of the Spirit. 2 For the law of the Spirit of life [which is] in Christ Jesus [the law of our new being] has freed me from the law of sin and of death. 3 For God has done what the Law could not do, [its power] being weakened by the flesh [the entire nature of man without the Holy Spirit]. Sending His own Son in the guise of sinful flesh and as an offering for sin, [God] condemned sin in the flesh [subdued, overcame, deprived it of its power over all who accept that sacrifice], 4 So that the righteous and just requirement of the Law might be fully met in us who live and move not in the ways of the flesh but in the ways of the Spirit [our lives governed not by the standards and according to the dictates of the flesh, but controlled by the Holy Spirit]. 5 For those who are according to the flesh and are controlled by its unholy desires set their minds on and pursue those things which gratify the flesh, but those who are according to the Spirit and are controlled by the desires of the Spirit set their minds on and seek those things which gratify the Spirit. 6 Now the mind of the flesh [which is sense and reason without the Holy Spirit] is death [death that comprises all the miseries arising from sin, both here and hereafter]. But the mind of the [Holy] Spirit is life and [soul] peace [both now and forever]. 7 [That is] because the mind of the flesh [with its carnal thoughts and purposes] is hostile to God, for it does not submit itself to God's Law; indeed it cannot. 8 So then those who are living the life of the flesh [catering to the appetites and impulses of their carnal nature] cannot please or satisfy God, or be acceptable to Him. 9 But you are not living the life of the flesh, you are living the life of the Spirit, if the [Holy] Spirit of God [really] dwells within you [directs and controls you]. But if anyone does not possess the [Holy] Spirit of Christ, he is none of His [he does not belong to Christ, is not truly a child of God]. 10 But if Christ lives in you, [then although] your [natural] body is dead by reason of sin and guilt, the spirit is alive because of [the] righteousness [that He imputes to you]. Holy Bible: Amplified (Kindle Locations 34076-34084). The Lockman Foundation. Kindle Edition.*

Study Notes: After taking a hard look at myself, and seeing where I was in the church. I felt a tugging of being more and more like Christ. Pastor Daryl Coley had sung this song, "To Be More Like Jesus." I was so moved by the worship that God had allowed me to be a part of in the Choir. Everyone that stood before us to teach in Music Ministry, had such a determination style in their worship. So my prayer went like this, "Lord show me You, help me to be more like You, so that I may worship You in Spirit and in Truth.

In Christ Jesus was the first line that leaped from the scriptur into my spirit. There was now no condemnation to those of us who were in Christ Jesus. The rest of verse one says, *"Who live [and] walk not after the dictates of the flesh, but after the dictates of the Spirit."*

1. There was a blessing in not living and walking after the dictates of the flesh. My flesh could not lead me to where my spirit desired to go.
2. Walking after my flesh meant that I would fall prey to the gratification and desires of my fleshly desires.
3. By verse 6, I had to sit up, walk around, and sit back down. For I realized that walking after the spirit instead of the flesh was a life and death situation and outcome.
4. I wanted to please God, and my feeling were so hurt for those who refuse the Holy Ghost in their lives. Verse 6 hit me like a ton of bricks, I literally got weak at the knees for some of my brothers and sisters. The Word said that if we have not the Holy Ghost that we are non of His.
   Thus, I desired more than anything to aquire more of Him.

My desire is to share Him so much the more, so that You would desire Him to. Verses *7 [That is] because the mind of the flesh [with its carnal thoughts and purposes] is hostile to God, for it does not submit itself to God's Law; indeed it cannot. 8 So then those who are living the life of the flesh [catering to the appetites and impulses of their carnal nature] cannot please or satisfy God, or be acceptable to Him.* The Amplified Translation of Scripture 81
has taught and inspired me on this kingdom walk.

These two verses were one of many that shed a lot into why and how to crucify my flesh for kingdom purposes. It enlightened me of how to view my flesh, and how to catagorize it verses my spirit.
I trust and pray that it will do the same for you, for this is a chiseling, and carving passage, the entire Chapter of Romans 8.
Digesting it will help to shape some of the ordered steps in this walk. You will understand as I did, exactly how much clout your flesh believes it has when it come to fighting against the spirit.
It caused the "element" in me to be ignited and burn with great fire, that fire being the Holy Ghost.

Days 7, 8, 9

Galatians 2:20-21

Prayer Focus: Precious Father, we come again in Your Matchless Name. We thank You for the precious gift of the Holy Ghost. We thank You for Your Blood. We thank You for life, health and strength. We glorify Your Name. We repent of anything that we may have said or done that was not pleasing in Your sight. I bless You as I journey into the experience of crucifying my flesh. I bless You as I render my life unto death that I may live You. Thank You for teaching me, leading me, instructing me into a sold out life. Help me to die daily, crucifying my flesh that I might walk fully surrendered unto You. I love You Lord, with my whole heart, Help me to be more like You. I bless You now and give You praise. In Your Name I do Pray, Amen.

Bible Reading: Galatians 2:20-21
20 I have been crucified with Christ [in Him I have shared His crucifixion]; it is no longer I who live, but Christ (the Messiah) lives in me; and the life I now live in the body I live by faith in (by adherence to and reliance on and complete trust in) the Son of God, Who loved me and gave Himself up for me. 21 [Therefore, I do not treat God's gracious gift as something of minor importance and defeat its very purpose]; I do not set aside and invalidate and frustrate and nullify the grace (unmerited favor) of God. For if justification (righteousness, acquittal from guilt) comes through [observing the ritual of] the Law, then Christ (the Messiah) died groundlessly and to no purpose and in vain. [His death was then wholly superfluous.] (2008-05-13). Holy Bible: Amplified (Kindle Locations 35558-35563). The Lockman Foundation. Kindle Edition. **83**

Study Notes: Our life is a crucified life. It is a life fully dedicated to the life of Christ. The life that we live is actually the life of Christ. So often we get tied up in our plans and our goals that we desire to meet. When in this passage there is a clear state that says, our life is crucified is killed, is hung on the cross with His life. We have no life outside of Christ. There is only two teams, there is only two captains. We cannot serve both. We can't live in the world and in Christ at the same time. Kingdom has been established, the church has been put into place, a life in Chirst has been ressurected. That life we now live is done so by faith in Jesus Christ. The Lord instructed me saying, Only In Christ, we stand Victorious, outside of Him, we are nothing. The life that we live in Him is a life of honor, sacrifice, dedication, commitment, consecration, and dignity. It is a life of excellency that can only be found in Christ.

Day 10,11,12

PRAYER FOCUS Precious Father, I come again thanking you for the precious Holy Spirit that You left to comfort, lead and guide us. Lord, I thank You for as I grow up in You that You have blessed me with what I need to become a tall stature, rooted and grounded in Your Love. I think You for demonstating to me through Your Word the ability to lean not to the works of the flesh, but be encouraged to walk after the gift of the Spirit. Lord, I ask that if there be anything in me that is not pleasing, show it to me, that I may avoid those activities that will separate me from You and ultimately find me with death for that is the wages of sin. Show me, that I may repent, turn and not operate with unseemly actions in my life. I thank You father for my goal is to spend an everlasting eternity with You. In Your Name I pray, Amen.

18 But if you are guided (led) by the [Holy] Spirit, you are not subject to the Law. 19 Now the doings (practices) of the flesh are clear (obvious): they are immorality, impurity, indecency, 20 Idolatry, sorcery, enmity, strife, jealousy, anger (ill temper), selfishness, divisions (dissensions), party spirit (factions, sects with peculiar opinions, heresies), 21 Envy, drunkenness, carousing, and the like. I warn you beforehand, just as I did previously, that those who do such things shall not inherit the kingdom of God. 22 But the fruit of the [Holy] Spirit [the work which His presence within accomplishes] is love, joy (gladness), peace, patience (an even temper, forbearance), kindness, goodness (benevolence), faithfulness, 23 Gentleness (meekness, humility), self-control (self-restraint, continence). Against such things there is no law [that can bring a charge]. 24 And those who belong to Christ Jesus (the Messiah) have crucified the flesh (the godless human nature) with its passions and appetites and desires. 25 If we live by the [Holy] Spirit, let us also walk by the Spirit. [If by the Holy Spirit we have our life in God, let us go forward walking in line, our conduct controlled by the Spirit.]

Holy Bible: Amplified (Kindle Location 35695). The Lockman Foundation. Kindle Edition.

Study Notes: The Prodominate take-away from this familiar passage found in Galatians 5, is that it is a great measuring device.

What do I mean by that, I found that as I visited this passage, I found issues that I had that definitely needed fixing and changing. I for one had a bad attitude, I had a smart mouth, and almost always, ended up in an argument or heated discussion. And would have to pray hard for an attitude adjustment.

I was guilty of having envy, strife, if we scan the list, I believe jealousy was the only work of the flesh that did not have a hold on me. But, I must say, that if were to scratch anything off the list it would be jealousy. I found out though, that they all entertwined, so scratching off was not an option. If one was in operation, then the rest were also.

Developing a consistent flow of the fruit of the Spirit in ones life is not hard at all. Why do I say that, once we realize who we are in Christ, and completely give ourselves over to Him, there comes a desire to please Him in all of our ways. With that, dedication, commitment will nag on our appetites until we give in to it's demand on our life.

A begin and continual "Yes" unto the Lord, will send us into a desire to fast, pray and seeking to be more like Him. It is falling in Love with Jesus. The more we give in to those fruits and have a desire to have them fully operating in our life, the less we will want to satisfy our ruthless flesh. When we talk to Him, He talks back. When we love on Him, He loves us first, then loves us back. Sometimes we can try to hard to do a thing. Let's rely on His Word and see what it says.

1. **Philippians 2:13** [Not in your own strength] for it is God Who is all the while effectually at work in you [energizing and creating in you the power and desire], both to will and to work for His good pleasure and satisfaction and delight. (2008-05-13). Holy Bible: Amplified (Kindle Locations 36024-36026). The Lockman Foundation. Kindle Edition.
2. **Colossians 2:6** As you have therefore received Christ, [even] Jesus the Lord, [so] walk (regulate your lives and conduct yourselves) in union with and conformity to Him. 7 Have the roots [of your being] firmly and deeply planted [in Him, fixed and founded in Him], being continually built up in Him, becoming increasingly more confirmed and established in the faith, just as you were taught, and abounding and overflowing in it with thanksgiving. (2008-05-13). Holy Bible: Amplified (Kindle Locations

176-36179). The Lockman Foundation. Kindle Edition.
3. **Jude 20** But you, beloved, build yourselves up [founded] on your most holy faith [make progress, rise like an edifice higher and higher], praying in the Holy Spirit; 21 Guard and keep yourselves in the love of God; expect and patiently wait for the mercy of our Lord Jesus Christ (the Messiah)—[which will bring you] unto life eternal. (2008-05-13). Holy Bible: Amplified (Kindle Locations 38028-38031). The Lockman Foundation. Kindle Edition.

These are three scriptures that encouraged me on kingdom walking. There are many, as you read these in your Bible, KJV, there will be references. God loves us so much, in spite of what some may say to detur us from living a Spirit filled life.

I'd admonish you not to give up nor give in. There is a great reward awaiting us as we follow the Spirit's lead. Allow Him to lead and guide us into all truths. Rendering or presenting our bodies to the Lord as a living sacrifice will pay off, and not just after awhile.

Repeating these twelve days at least once a month will equal one-hundred and forty-four days of consecration. It's good to spiritually clean out our own house, laying ourselves on the altar. There is a shifting or quickening that takes place in our total being as we stand victoriously in Christ. Keeping our vessels clean is a job, it becomes easier as we allow our total being to be aligned with God's will. He is our help, looking to the heals become a must as we put our trust in the true and living God.

I believe there is a scripture that says, we are to look unto Jesus, who is the author and finisher of our faith. (Hebrews 12:2) He is well able to keep us from falling (failing/stumbling). (Jude 24-25)

The true victory is resting in His grace. He assures us grace and mercy. His ultimate goal is that we through Him be sanctified wholly, body, soul, and spirit and be found blameless until He comes.

References

Kindle Books

2015/From the Prayer Warriors and Intercessors Handbook, Ambassador Black

2008-05-13). Holy Bible: Amplified (Kindle Locations 35558-35563). The Lockman Foundation. Kindle Edition

(Strongs Concordance)

Dedications

Some of My Cheereleaders

Mr. Luther Stephney, My Dad

In Memory of my mom, Ms. Cora Mae Pruitt-Cureton

Bishop Jimmy and Co-Pastor, Evangelist Shirley Magee. House of Prayer Apostolic Church, Laurel, MS

Evangelist Hilda Cooley, For the Love of God Deliverance Ministry, Laurel, MS

Bishop Sean & Apostle Melissa Mapp, (My Pastors) Greater Mission International Ministry, Laurel, MS

My Husband & My Children and their families, Elder Pete Black, Sanu Amen, Donnell Vaughn, Shontina Jackson, and Thynell Black

Pastor Cornelius McDonald, St. John the Baptist Church-Heidlcbcrg,   **89**

Pastor Alice Nelson, Restoration Life Church, Laurel, MS

Evangelisgt Naomi Bush, Bishop Abraham Yarbrough, Sr., Elder Harvey Yarbrough, Greater Trueway Apostolic Church-Hattiesburg, MS

Pastor Betty Grant and Mountain Top Ministry of Broadheadsville, Pennsylvania

My brothers and sisters, Willie James Pruitt, Robin Roberts, Kathy Torrence-Taylor, William Elijah Pruitt, Yuka Stephney, Luther Stephney, Jr.

And many others who have supported us in ministry with prayers and patronage

Made in the USA
Columbia, SC
16 July 2022